AMERI

EMPIRE

BEFORE THE FALL

D0384299

BRUCE FEIN

Cover Illustration: Christopher Heirs
Art Direction: Matthew Holdridge
Editor: Daniel McCarthy
Marketing and Publishing Manager: Gary Howard Jr.

ISBN: 1452829535
ISBN-13: 9781452829531

This book is dedicated to Socrates, who preferred death to the unexamined life.

Acknowledgements

I would like to acknowledge the untiring assistance of my Executive Assistant Derek Scott Richardson in preparing the manuscript. Mr. Richardson played a pivotal editorial role. He worked nights and on weekends when needed. He served as a sounding board in refining ideas and themes. He offered ideas for chapter titles, organization, and the book cover. He was a Patroclus to Achilles.

I further express my appreciation for Mary Feamster, Seunghee Seo, and Meaghan McGrath of the Rutherford Institute in preparing the footnotes.

Foreword

In this compelling review of world history and American foreign policy, Bruce Fein reminds us that great nations who do not temper their global ambitions do not remain great for long. Rome, the British Colonial Empire, and the Soviet Union all buckled under the strain of their efforts to extend their influence abroad.

American Empire underscores the fact that if the United States means to remain the most powerful nation in the world, we cannot continue to borrow and spend – mortgaging our children's future – to supply infrastructure, government, and aid to other parts of the world.

Fein also gives us an in-depth look at the abdication of U.S. Congressional power to the Executive branch. The Congress has, over time, shirked its responsibility to declare war, rein in government spending, and challenge the President when he oversteps his authority. Now, as the U.S. government expands its control over the American people by way of new government programs and entitlements, the Congress must push back. As Fein points out, 'government is more the problem than the solution.'

Finally, *American Empire* examines another aspect of contemporary American life: the balance between security and freedom. The national debate over whether we are willing to compromise our civil liberties – our rights to free speech, due process, property and privacy – in an effort to protect ourselves from harm persists. How do we remain secure from threats abroad and at home without giving way to unbridled government control?

What does history tell us about what trade-offs the 'protected' must make to enable the 'protector'? And, can we, as a people, ever be truly 'secure' when our 'freedom' is infringed upon?

Fein astutely notes: "History teaches that nations do not learn from history." *American Empire*'s thorough review of past world powers' mistakes gives our nation the opportunity to avoid repeating them.

- *Congressman Walter B. Jones*
(04/20/2010)

Contents

1

Empire Without a Cause

It is the best of times for the American Empire.
It is the worst of times for the American Republic.

You, your family, your friends, your professional colleagues, and your elected and appointed officials in the nation's highest circles will fiercely resist the truths this book expounds. Your vocation will seem less important or grand when measured against the American Republic's revolutionary creed and the Founding Fathers' conception of civic virtue. Your pride in the United States as the world's sole superpower will be challenged. Your instinct to equate national security or divine uplift with the export of democracy or human rights abroad will be discredited. Your orthodoxies which evoke pride in the United States for bestriding the globe like a military colossus will be upended. But you will find comfort in the knowledge that your skepticism of the ideas you will encounter is widely shared.

We, the current citizens of the United States, have all been raised to embrace the American Empire without questioning its premises, just as British subjects more than a century ago viscerally cherished and celebrated the British Empire. The justifications for Empires are characteristically unexamined to conceal an unflattering truth: they are all fueled by a base, animalistic craving to dominate other nations and people for the sake of domination.

Acclaimed Austrian scholar Joseph Schumpeter captured the essence of Empire in his 1919 description of Imperialism in *The Sociology of Imperialism:*

> For whenever the word "imperialism" is used, there is always the implication—whether sincere or not—of an aggressiveness, the true reasons for which do not lie in the aims which are temporarily being pursued; of an aggressiveness that is only kindled anew by each success; of an aggressiveness for its own sake, as reflected in such terms as "hegemony," "world dominion," and so forth. And history, in truth, shows us nations and classes—most nations furnish an example at some time or other—that seek expansion for the sake of expanding, war for the sake of fighting, victory for the sake of winning, dominion for the sake of ruling. This determination cannot be explained by any of the pretexts that bring it into action, by any of the aims for which it seems to be struggling at the time. It confronts us, independent of all concrete purpose or occasion, as an enduring disposition, seizing upon one opportunity as eagerly as the next. It shines through all the arguments put forward on behalf of present aims. It values conquest not so much on account of the immediate advantages—advantages that more often than not are more than dubious, or that are heedlessly cast away with the same frequency—as because it is conquest, success, action...Expansion for its own sake always requires, among other things, concrete objects if it is to reach the action stage and maintain itself, but this does not

constitute its meaning. Such expansion is in a sense its own "object," and the truth is that it has no adequate object beyond itself...It may sound paradoxical, but numberless wars—perhaps the majority of all wars—have been waged without adequate "reason..."[1]

Earmarks of the American Empire, which corroborate Schumpeter, are legion.

In the American Republic, the law was king. In the American Empire, the President is law.

After 9/11, both President George W. Bush and President Barack Obama claimed unchecked authority to assassinate any American suspected of creating a "constant" and "imminent" danger to United States interests abroad.[2] President Bush was advised by the Department of Justice that his Commander in Chief powers enabled him to massacre civilians in the alleged "war" on international terrorism.[3]

President Obama asserts that the provision of legal services on behalf of a listed foreign terrorist organization or a specially designated global terrorist to challenge the constitutionality of the listings or designations is itself a federal felony, i.e., asserting innocence of endangering national security is a crime! Punishing lawyers for providing legal representation is what partially condemns Russia and China as tyrannies. Indeed, Nazi lawyers in the post-war Nuremberg Justice Cases were prosecuted for complicity in a decree of May 21, 1942, which stipulated, "that in accordance with the order on penal justice in Poland of 4 December 1941 attorneys are not (to) undertake the defense of Polish persons before tribunals in the incorporated Eastern territories." Due process in the American Empire has reverted to the legally primitive days before Magna Carta in 1215.

Anything done in the name of defeating international terrorism is legal. President Bush is advised that his powers as Commander in Chief supersede *any* limitation enacted by Congress if the presidential lawlessness is thought helpful to thwarting jihadists, including prohibitions of torture, kidnapping, or even homicide.

Government lawlessness is no longer news, like the rising and setting of the sun. The FBI illegally collected more than 2,000 U.S. telephone call records between 2002 and 2006 by invoking bogus terrorism emergencies or persuading phone companies to cooperate in violation of the Electronic Communications Privacy Act. No FBI agent is sanctioned.

President Bush and his national security circle flouted the criminal prohibitions of the Foreign Intelligence Surveillance Act for more than five years by intercepting the phone calls or emails of American citizens on American soil without a judicial warrant. No criminal investigation ensued. Waterboarding, i.e., torture, likewise goes unprosecuted. Neither the attorneys who concocted legal justifications for the crime nor doctors who participated in the interrogation abuses nor government officials who authorized the same are sanctioned.

Former Secretary of the Treasury, Henry Paulson, sworn to uphold and defend the Constitution, boasted that he showered billions of taxpayer dollars on failing financial institutions without a crumb of legal authority, yet encountered no repercussions.[4]

President Barack Obama has followed if not bettered the national security instruction of the Bush-Cheney duumvirate, confounding messianic expectations.

His 2010 Nobel Peace Prize address boasted of the American Empire's six decades of policing the world and of his unchecked power, reminiscent of British Kings, to commence war in ostensible defense of the United States or for professed humanitarian purposes on his say-so alone. President Obama emphasized: "I—like any head of state—reserve the right to act unilaterally if necessary to defend my nation."[5] The President spoke while he unilaterally expanded United States wars in Afghanistan and Pakistan against peoples unthreatening to United States sovereignty

More than 100,000 American troops are fighting in Iraq while civil war or partition looms in the wake of the acrimonious elections of

EMPIRE WITHOUT A CAUSE

March 2010. An indefinite military presence is planned there in hopes of stabilizing the region.

The post-9/11 perpetual and global war against international terrorism continues unabated. The United States claims unique legal power to violate the sovereignty of every foreign country with predator drones, missile strikes, or foot soldiers in seeking to capture or kill an Al Qaeda suspect.

United States weapons, money, Special Forces, military advisors, and professed nation-building bureaucrats are poised to intervene in Yemen in response to a foiled Christmas day attempt to blow up a commercial aircraft by a Muslim youth who may have been radicalized there. Secretary of State Hillary Clinton worries that, "The instability in Yemen is a threat to regional stability and even global stability."[6] The Chairman of the Senate Homeland Security Committee, Joe Lieberman (Ind. Conn.), declared the incident an act of *war* that requires a *military,* not a law enforcement, response—like fighting the Nazi Luftwaffe or Emperor Hirohito's Zero aircraft in World War II. He urges that the would-be suicide bomber, 23-year-old Umar Farouk Abdulmutullab, be regarded as a prisoner of war and prosecuted before a military commission denuded of ordinary due process protections.[7]

After Yemen, Somalia is in the queue to be invaded by the American Empire because of collaboration between the Somali terrorist organization Al Shabab and Al Qaeda in the Arabian Peninsula. War ineluctably expands to wherever a terrorist may dwell.

Exponents of the Empire falsely assert that critical intelligence will be frustrated if suspected terrorists are criminally prosecuted because defense lawyers will advise silence. In obtaining more than 200 terrorist-related convictions since 9/11, criminal defendants have regularly provided counterterrorism intelligence to obtain leniency or otherwise. In November 2009, federal prosecutors in Minneapolis unsealed criminal charges against eight Somali men who had served as recruiters, sending area youths from the Twin Cities into Africa to serve as suicide bombers. The prosecution's case was assembled with help from suspects who had been quietly cooperating with authorities.

AMERICAN EMPIRE: BEFORE THE FALL

A Chicago suspect, after detention at O'Hare International Airport, exposed fresh details of the 2008 plot to bomb hotels, a train station and a Jewish cultural center in Mumbai. David Coleman Headley has pleaded guilty to criminal involvement in the plot, and is cooperating with prosecutors.

Bryant Neal Vinas, a former New York City transit worker and convert to Islam, provided U.S. and Belgian law enforcement with a deeper understanding of Al Qaeda training camps and testified in European courts against fellow trainees, according to court papers.

The incentive to talk in exchange for reduced criminal charges or punishment is enormous. Abdulmutullab continues to talk to the FBI despite receiving Miranda warnings and retaining an attorney.

Tiny Denmark, whose defense budget is a decimal point of the Pentagon's, is less easily frightened than the United States. On January 1, 2010, a Somali Muslim attempted to assassinate artist Kurt Westergaard in revenge for a 2005 cartoon depicting the Prophet Mohammad as a terrorist. The portrayal had earlier provoked Muslim firebombing attacks on Danish diplomatic missions and three other radical Islamic plots to kill the Danish cartoonist. Denmark's intelligence chief asserted the assassination incident was "terrorist related," with a possible connection to Al Shabab.[8] The Danish Prime Minister descried the terrorism as "an attack on our open society and our democracy."[9] Yet Denmark did not declare war on terrorism or against Al Shabab. It did not declare the would-be assassin a prisoner of war or slate him for trial before a military commission. The Danish government arrested and charged the accused with attempted murder subject to prosecution in civilian courts with customary due process protections. The easily alarmed American Empire, in contrast, would have condemned the attempted assassination as an act of war subject to prosecution before a military tribunal.

Fright and expense prompted the Obama administration to abandon a federal criminal prosecution of Khalid Sheik Mohammad, mastermind of the 9/11 abominations, in New York City.

The United States has never been safer from existential threats. Yet Americans are inundated with an endless stream of fear-inducing stories featured in leading newspapers and broadcasts. As Scott Shane in *The New York Times* has written (January 13, 2010):

> As terrorist plots against the United States have piled up in recent months, politicians and the news media have sounded the alarm with a riveting message for Americans: Be afraid. Al Qaeda is on the march again, targeting the country from within and without, and your hapless government cannot protect you. But the politically charged clamor has lumped together disparate cases and obscured the fact that the enemies on American soil in 2009…were a scattered, uncoordinated group of amateurs who displayed more fervor than skill…Exactly 14 of the approximately 14,000 murders in the United States resulted from allegedly jihadist attacks: 13 people shot at Fort Hood in Texas in November and one at a military recruiting station in Little Rock, Ark., in June.[10]

In contrast, 21 were murdered at Virginia Tech by a mentally imbalanced student in 2007.

The American Empire's exaggerations corroborate General Douglas MacArthur's post-World War II observation: "Our economy is now geared to an arms economy bred in an artificially induced psychosis of war hysteria and an incessant propaganda of fear."[11] Fear is chronically brandished by demagogic leaders to coax the masses to accept anything in the name of safety. H.L. Mencken elaborated in 1918: "Civilization, in fact, grows more and more maudlin and hysterical; especially under democracy it tends to degenerate into a mere combat of crazes; the whole aim of practical politics is to keep the populace alarmed (and hence clamorous to be led to safety) by an endless series of hobgoblins, most of them imaginary."[12]

AMERICAN EMPIRE: BEFORE THE FALL

The Founding Fathers would be appalled by the American Empire. They had constructed an American Republic to repudiate crusades, constant warfare or virtual deification of the President. They had pledged their lives, fortunes, and sacred honor to defeat the British Empire that featured global military tentacles, an unchecked executive, secrecy, and ubiquitous government regulation or protectionism. President Thomas Jefferson's First Inaugural Address proclaimed: "Peace, commerce, and honest friendship with all nations—entangling alliances with none."[13] President Grover Cleveland elaborated on the foreign policy of the United States inherited from the Constitution's makers:

> It is the policy of peace suitable to our interests. It is the policy of neutrality; rejecting any share in foreign brawls and ambitions on other continents, and repelling their intrusion here. It is the policy of Monroe and of Washington and Jefferson....[14]

The Founding Fathers' handiwork has turned to ashes. The vast majority of Americans irrespective of political persuasion unthinkingly assume that the United States should project itself into every nook and cranny of the globe to bolster national security and freedom by guaranteeing international stability and giving birth to new democracies. President Barack Obama, speaking at West Point on December 1, 2009, insisted that the United States has fought and will continue to fight for a better future for our children and grandchildren, whose future, in turn, depends on *other people* living in freedom and opportunity. In other words, the United States must fight to purge the world of tyranny and to prevent retrogression (as from Russia's Boris Yeltsin to Vladimir Putin) because freedom for Americans requires liberty throughout the planet!

That moral conviction stems partially from the Empire's self-righteousness. President Dwight D. Eisenhower sermonized: "America is great because she is good, and if America ever ceases to be good, she will cease to be great."[15]

Animated by a combination of moral and national security fervor, the Empire sports a military presence in 135 countries hosting more than 400,000 United States troops. Tens of thousands are abroad to defend the people and interests of South Korea, Japan, Europe, Afghanistan, Iraq, Saudi Arabia, etc. American soldiers are risking that last full measure of devotion not to secure the blessings of liberty to ourselves and our posterity, but to protect foreigners who pay no American taxes and have no American loyalties. German sage and unsentimental Prime Minister Otto von Bismarck knew better than to risk the lives of German soldiers for the sake of world domination. He preached: "The Balkans aren't worth the life of a single Pomeranian soldier."[16] The American Empire, however, militarily intervened in Bosnia in 1995 and Serbia-Kosovo in 1998 despite their irrelevance to American liberties or sovereignty. Both Bosnia and Kosovo remain de facto portioned along ethnic lines more than a decade later.

Article V of the NATO treaty, a product of America's psychology of Empire, absurdly commits the United States to defend from war all 27 other members, including Poland, the Czech Republic, the Slovak Republic, Hungary, Albania, Croatia, Lithuania, Latvia, and Estonia. But not a single NATO member's alliance is necessary to defend the sovereignty of the United States or the freedoms of its citizens. If every NATO member were conquered by a foreign foe, the United States would not be endangered.

Yet if Russia were to invade Hungary as in 1956, or the Czech and Slovak Republics as in 1969, the United States would be at war. Its soldiers would be dispatched to die for Hungarians, Czechs, and Slovaks. If international terrorists committed a series of attacks against France, Italy, or Bulgaria, the United States would be at war to defend them, just as the United States insisted that NATO countries assist militarily in defeating Al Qaeda after 9/11 under Article V.

NATO was born 60 years ago in 1949 to confront the now-dismembered Soviet Union in the Cold War. It responded to the Soviet de facto control of Eastern and Central Europe in contravention of the Yalta Accords and to the Berlin blockade that curtailed Allied land access to West Berlin. The United States feared that Western Europe might be overrun by the Soviet Union or become "Finlandized" without a defense pact. But even if those fears had been realized, the sovereignty or prosperity of the United States would not have been threatened. In 1949, the United States enjoyed a monopoly of atomic weaponry. It was by far the wealthiest nation in the world. Only a tiny fraction of the United States economy depended on foreign trade. United States military and civilian wartime casualties were 418,000 compared with a figure exceeding 23 million for the Soviet Union. No foreign nation was threatening to attack the United States or had the capability of doing so. Even if they had, the United States would not have needed the assistance of any other country to defend itself. The same is even truer today.

At present, several nations enjoying Article 5's protective umbrella might plausibly be engulfed in war with non-NATO countries in the foreseeable future, triggering United States involvement. Estonia, Latvia, and Lithuania could be attacked by Russia. The three host substantial ethnic Russian populations attached to the Russian language, Russian culture, and Russian war memorials. The loyalties of Russians are suspect in the three Baltic States. They were annexed by the Soviet Union from 1940 until its disintegration in 1991. The last Russian troops did not depart until 1994. Over 30% of Estonia's population is ethnic Russian. The corresponding figure for Latvia is 34%. Lithuania's Russian ethnics are a much smaller 6.3%. In 1994, to punish its former Latvian and Estonian colonies for allegedly mistreating their Russian minorities, and Lithuania for refusing to legitimate Russia's right of military transit to and from the enclave of Kaliningrad, Moscow resorted to economic blackmail. The Russian government levied prohibitive tariffs on imports of Baltic goods and raised prices on Russian fuel and other essential commodities. On or about May 2007, Russia looked the other way when a cyber-attack against Estonia was launched from within its borders. These actions spurred efforts by the three countries to mitigate their geopolitical and economic vulnerability through the development of stronger relationships with the West. There is a non-trivial possibility of a clash between Russia and one or more of the Baltic States in the next decades. Article 5 would compel intervention by the United States military in their defense despite their irrelevance to United States security.

If they were re-annexed by Russia, the latter's threat to the United States would not intensify. During the Cold War or earlier annexations to the Soviet Union, Estonia, Latvia, and Lithuania were ciphers in the balance of terror or mutually assured destruction between the rival superpowers. Their populations are 1.3 million, 2.2 million, and 3.3 million, respectively. They are militarily inconsequential. They are highly nationalistic, and were leaders in declaring independence from the Soviet Union. Russian military occupation would be resisted and would squander billions of rubles. The resulting strife would lessen Russia's ability to confront the United States militarily.

Albania might be drawn into a war initiated by Serbia or Macedonia despite Albania's invisibility on the United States national security landscape. Kosovo might turn to Albania for help if Serbia annexed Kosovo's secessionist Serb enclave. Macedonia's Albanians might similarly call for an Albanian rescue mission if Macedonia's majority becomes more oppressive.

The United States is urging NATO admissions for Georgia and Ukraine. Both are at risk of war with Russia. In 2008, Russia fought Georgia over the break-away territory of South Ossetia. Russia has formally recognized the independence of both South Ossetia and Abkhazia from Georgia. It kept troops in Georgian territory in violation of last year's cease-fire accord over South Ossetia. Moreover, it has established a military base in Abkhazia. Georgia's volatile President, Mikhail Saakashvilli, might exploit NATO membership to provoke Russia to war. Saakashvilli probably initiated the clash over South Ossetia to accelerate Georgia's NATO bid. A Russian conquest of Georgia would not heighten Russia's national security threat to the United States. It would tie the Russian army down with a restive Georgian population reminiscent of Russia's quagmire in Chechnya, and similarly squander billions of rubles.

Ukraine-Russian relations have historically been tense, and could erupt in armed conflict despite the recent 2010 election of Ukraine President Viktor Yankovych pledged to amity. Russian ethnics concentrated in the east constitute 17.3% of the population. Ukrainian politics split sharply on an East-West divide, which finds expression in the rancor over Russia's leased naval base at Sevastopol on the Black Sea, scheduled to expire in 2017.[17]

Why should the United States be militarily bound under Article V to defend Ukraine from Russian conquest? With or without Ukraine, Russia does not threaten the sovereignty of the United States or the liberties of its people. That the United States would even contemplate, not to say encourage, the admission of Ukraine into NATO is indicative of the American Empire's instinct for world domination.

And what national security sense does it make for the United States to defend Croatia if it were attacked by Serbia over a border dispute, or by Russia as an ally of Serbia? If Croatia were swallowed by either, the effect on the liberty, safety, or welfare of Americans would be submicroscopic. Croatia, moreover, can contribute nothing to deterring or retaliating against an attack on the United States. The argument that Russia would become a greater threat to the United States by conquering Croatia is nonsense. Croats would resist Russian troops like Afghans resisted the Soviet invasion in 1979 or like the Chechens opposed the Russian army in the First and Second Chechen Wars. The Russian military would be harassed and vexed by seething Croats. During World War II, the Roman Catholic Croats fought the Orthodox Serbs and Soviet forces as an independent fascist state under the Ustasha organization.

Russia's encounter with the Chechen resistance in the Second Chechen War is instructive of how Russia might fare in Croatia. Even after victory, tens of thousands of Russian troops remained years later to provide security. Chechnya is an economic albatross. It earns only 5% of its budget. The remainder comes from Moscow. Russia subsidizes Chechnya to the tune of over $1 billion annually. A Russian conquest of Croatia would probably curtail, not enhance its danger to the United States.

EMPIRE WITHOUT A CAUSE

The United States is saddled with defense obligations that correspond to Article V of the NATO Charter with South Korea and Japan. But neither country is relevant to preserving United States sovereignty or the individual liberties of its citizens.

Other nations are eager for the United States to pay for and to die in their defense. As President Obama bugled in his December 1, 2009, West Point address, "But more than any other nation, the United States of America has underwritten global security for over six decades...."[18]

Preemptive war and global domination have become fixtures of the American Empire. A 1992 draft of a Defense Department document authored by then Under Secretary of Defense for Policy, Paul Wolfowitz, championed the use of the military in the post-Cold War era "to prevent the re-emergence of a new rival."[19] In 1997, conservative William Kristol and Robert Kagan founded "Project for the New American Century" (PNAC), a Washington-based think tank. PNAC attracted Wolfowitz, future Vice President Dick Cheney, future Secretary of Defense Donald Rumsfeld, and future member of the Defense Advisory Board, Richard Perle. Citing a concern for "isolationist impulses" and neglect of a strategic vision for America's role in the world, PNAC trumpeted:

> ...we cannot safely avoid the responsibilities of global leadership or the costs that are associated with its exercise. America has a vital role in maintaining peace and security in Europe, Asia, and the Middle East. If we shirk our responsibilities, we invite challenges to our fundamental interests...
>
> [1] we need to increase defense spending significantly if we are to carry out our global responsibilities today and modernize our armed forces for the future; [2] we need to strengthen our ties to democratic allies and to challenge regimes hostile to our interests and values; [3] we need to promote the cause of political

and economic freedom abroad; [4] we need to accept responsibility for America's unique role in preserving and extending an international order friendly to our security, our prosperity and our principles.[20]

A 2000 PNAC paper also advocated military control of the Persian Gulf region featuring regime change in Iraq in an overall strategy. It described United States forces in foreign lands as "the cavalry on the new American frontier."[21] New York Times bestselling author William Rivers Pitt aptly described the institution's vaulting ambitions, writing: "Above all else, the PNAC desires and demands one thing: The establishment of a global American empire to bend the will of all nations."[22]

The PNAC's celebration of a global military footprint and domination was no aberration. It reflected the American Empire's political culture. Two days after the 9/11 abominations, then Defense Secretary Wolfowitz explained that the war against international terrorism would entail "removing the sanctuaries, removing the support systems, ending states who sponsor terrorism" [like Syria, Libya, Cuba, Sudan, Iraq, and Iran].[23] On June 1, 2002, President George W. Bush saluted preemptive war as a cornerstone of the American Empire: "[O]ur security will require all Americans to be forward-looking and resolute, to be ready for preemptive action when necessary to defend our liberty and to defend our lives."[24]

The Bush-Cheney ambitions are thriving. The imperative of preemptive wars to defeat international terrorism is championed by liberal and conservative minds alike. Look no further than President Obama's Nobel Peace Prize speech, escalation of the Afghan war into Pakistan, and minatory gestures towards Yemen and Iran.

The American Empire's annual military national security budget, including the intelligence agencies and nuclear weapons programs of the Department of Energy, approximate $1 trillion. That figure vastly exceeds the yearly military expenditures of the next 25 countries combined.

President Obama predictably has exempted the Defense Department from the spending freeze imposed on domestic programs. United States military spending climbs despite the disappearance of all foreign dangers to United States sovereignty.

The defense budget of Russia, a superpower rival of the United States as the U.S.S.R. until 1991, has dwindled to a small fraction of the Pentagon's. It is not an existential or even semi-existential threat. The safety of the United States does not turn on mutually assured destruction. Russia's armed forces are a shadow of the Soviet Red Army. Its military struggles to defeat primitive Islamic forces in Chechnya, Dagestan, and Ingushetia. The Beslan school terrorist massacre in North Ossetia-Alani, in which over 1,000 were killed or injured, is illustrative of Russia's jihadist cancer. During its clash with Georgia over South Ossetia in 2008, United States ships carried civilian aid to Georgians through the Black Sea undisturbed by the Russian navy. Russia's population is plunging towards 100 million, and the average longevity of its citizens has fallen to 67, lower than Iraq's.

Russia chronically disputes with China over the Ussuri River border and with Japan over the Kurile Islands. Its oil and gas dependent economy has shriveled as the price of energy has tumbled and Russia's notorious lawlessness has frightened off foreign investors.

Senator John McCain's exhortation that "we are all Georgians now" in his 2008 presidential campaign absurdly inflated the military threat of Russia a thousand fold, akin to Don Quixote's tilting at windmills.[25] The former POW hoped to evoke President John F. Kennedy's soaring oratory in Berlin on June 26, 1963: "Two thousand years ago the proudest boast was 'civis Romanus sum.' Today, in the world of freedom, the proudest boast is 'Ich bin ein Berliner.'"[26] McCain's analogy did not wash.

Georgia's democratic credentials paled in comparison to West Berlin's. Georgia's headstrong President, Mikheil Saakashvilli, initiated or provoked the conflict. And Russia's armed forces were no threat to Western Europe—and certainly not to the United States—in contrast to the menacing Soviet Red Army in East Berlin in 1963.

McCain's "the sky is falling" nonsense escaped derision by peers, the media, and the American public. Indeed, among others, then Chairman of the Senate Foreign Relations Committee, Joseph Biden (D. Del), and then Vice President Dick Cheney raced to the region to promise Georgia lavish United States military and economic support. Like McCain, they fatuously insisted that saving Georgia's semi-authoritarian government from Russian danger was indispensable to America's sovereignty and freedom.

The United States hyper-alarm at the Russia-South Ossetia-Georgia jousting illustrated the American Empire's psychology in full blossom. It viscerally exaggerates danger from abroad to frighten the people into saluting a global military footprint, yielding their civil liberties, indulging secret over transparent government, and conferring on the President omnipotent military and economic power. These defilements of the American Republic are perpetrated in a fruitless quest for absolute safety and for the juvenile thrill of dominating others.

Fear that China will soon rival or surpass the United States in military or economic power or global influence is fanciful. China is handicapped by internal upheavals. Tibetans, lead by the Dalai Lama from Dharamsala, India, insist on genuine autonomy or independence. Military clashes in Lhasa and rebellion by Buddhist monks there are chronic. In East Turkestan, or Xinjiang Province, in the northeast, China confronts a seething Uighur community of 20 million. Lead by Nobel Peace Prize nominee Rebiya Kadeer, Uighurs demand an autonomous or separate state to protect their identity and culture from destruction by a mushrooming number of non-indigenous Han Chinese.

The 2008 Beijing Olympics bespoke the lingering insecurity of the Chinese Communist Party born of its fragile legitimacy—an anxiety still heightened by the Tiananmen Square Massacre of 1989. All who sought registration to protest against the Chinese government during the games in one of three zones set aside for dissidents were either arrested or deported. Chinese authorities sentenced two women in their 70s to a year's "re-education through labor" after they applied to protest the confiscation of their properties. Chinese dissidents routinely disappear into secret jails as retaliation for petitioning the Chinese Communist Party for redress of grievances, including freedom of speech, free elections, or corrupt police.

In March 2009, the second ranking Chinese Communist Party official stated to the National People's Congress that China would never embrace western style democracy, and that the CCP's method of representing the people was superior to representation through popular elections. The CCP worried over several anniversaries in 2009 that could have sparked mass demonstrations: the student-led protest of imperial rule in 1919, the birth of the People's Republic of China in 1949, the Tibet uprising of 1959 sponsored by the Dali Lama, the Tiananmen Square massacre of 1989, and the suppression of the Falun Gong in 1999.

China's relations with Vietnam are tense. China fought a brief border war against Vietnam in 1979, but was smartly rebuffed. At present, China routinely kills Vietnamese who stray into its territorial waters. China quarrels with India over a border that precipitated war in 1962. It fumes over the Dalai Lama's hosting at Dharamsala, and contests with India over influence in South Asia by, among other things, supporting Pakistan over Kashmir. China clashes with Japan over territory and maritime rights, and Japan's euphemistic descriptions of the Rape of Nanking. China worries about a democratic culture in Hong Kong infecting the mainland. It is daunted by the prospect of enormous casualties if it attempts the conquest of Taiwan.

China is no threat to United States sovereignty or the individual liberties of American citizens. It has never attacked United States territory (China sent hundreds of thousands of soldiers to assist North Korea in the Korean War at a time when the United States was flirting with an attack on China). And China's nuclear arsenal is light-years behind the United States.

James Madison, father of the Constitution and the Bill of Rights, prophetically warned more than two centuries ago: "The means of defense against foreign danger historically have become the instruments of tyranny at home."[27] But the American Empire, like the French Bourbons, forgets nothing and learns nothing.

AMERICAN EMPIRE: BEFORE THE FALL

The Empire psychology shuns inquiry into whether world domination by force of arms augments national security. Its orthodoxies are gospel shielded from debate. They are blind to the obvious: that indiscriminately seeking to suppress or eliminate every conceivable potential danger creates new enemies, squanders military resources that should be exclusively devoted to defending Americans at home, and cripples the rule of law. The idea and practice of neutrality or disinterestedness in foreign conflicts—the leitmotiv of President George Washington's Farewell Address—has been retired from public discourse.

During the golden era of the Republic, President Washington proclaimed United States neutrality in 1793 when Great Britain and France were at war. The United States remained scrupulously neutral when Central and South America were in upheaval against Spain and Portugal from 1809-1829.

In contrast, the American Empire concocts national security worries from trifles as light as air to justify United States intervention for the psychic thrill of power and the optics of safety. Nothing is too insignificant to attract United States military attention and concern, if not intervention. Puny conflicts between Russia and Ukraine over gas prices or the Black Sea port at Sevastopol, the Lord's Resistance Army in Uganda, mass killings in Darfur, the fate of Kosovar Albanians in Serbia or the Karen in Myanmar, a handful of adolescent Al Qaeda followers in Mali or Mauretania, Maoist terrorism in Nepal, Somalia's two decades of anarchy and the Shebab terrorist organization, Abu Sayyaf in the Philippines, a border dispute between Eritrea and Ethiopia, AIDS, crimes against humanity in Sudan, and a potential refugee crisis in Bangladesh that could be occasioned by global warming are all now designated as national security threats.

The wars in Afghanistan, Iraq, and against international terrorism are wars of choice, not of necessity. They sacrifice the lives and limbs of American soldiers while making the United States *less safe* and its citizens *less free*.

The wars deploy hundreds of thousands of troops abroad to fight aimlessly. United States soldiers were initially dispatched to Afghanistan to oust Taliban and to transform Afghanistan's primitive sectarian, tribal, and patriarchal culture into a thriving, secular, popular democracy at supersonic speed. That utopian objective predictably collided with President Hamid Karzai's complicity in massive voting fraud; ubiquitous corruption, including his brother's drug trafficking; alliances with war criminals; spiraling opium production; a law reducing women to chattels; and a tribal, ethnic, and sectarian political culture hostile to freedom of speech, freedom of religion, freedom of association, and due process of law. The President and Congress are now speechless about what victory means in Afghanistan beyond, "We'll know it when we see it."

The war in Iraq was first fought over non-existent weapons of mass destruction. It then morphed into a war for democracy, followed by a war to make Iraq less despotic than Saddam Hussein's tyranny. At present, President Obama cannot articulate the United States military objective in Iraq, indicative of an indefinite American troop presence there as in South Korea, Japan, or Germany. In the meantime, America has spent $1 trillion on operations and related defense spending for Iraq, and will be required to spend $2 trillion more to pay the war debt, replenish military equipment, and provide care and treatment for U.S. veterans.[28] Disability rates for veterans will grow higher for decades, as many will require indefinite care for brain and spinal injuries. Soldier stresses have occasioned a suicide rate amongst Army personnel at its highest peak since record keeping began.

At Gettysburg, President Abraham Lincoln explained the Civil War's aims that all could readily appreciate:

> The brave men, living and dead, who struggled here, have consecrated it, far above our poor power to add or detract. The world will little note, nor long remember what we say here, but it can never forget what they did here. It is for us the living, rather, to be dedicated here to the unfinished work which they who fought here have

thus far so nobly advanced. It is rather for us to be here dedicated to the great task remaining before us—that from these honored dead we take increased devotion to that cause for which they gave the last full measure of devotion—that we here highly resolve that these dead shall not have died in vain—that this nation, under God, shall have a new birth of freedom—and that government of the people, by the people, for the people, shall not perish from the earth.[29]

There will be no Gettysburg Address for the soldiers who perish in Afghanistan. None can explain why they fought or are fighting there except that they are obliged to follow orders. As with the Vietnam debacle, United States failures in Afghanistan breed more of the same flawed strategy, aping the stupidities of the British and Soviet Empires: more troops, more money, and more schoolmarm-like lectures about the urgency of political reform nurtured by military instructors. The same can be said for Iraq.

The American Empire's perpetual war with international terrorism conceives the globe (including the United States) as a battlefield where military force may be employed and military law may be imposed upon any person the President decrees is an Al Qaeda suspect. Military commissions that combine judge, jury, and prosecutor, secret evidence, and coerced testimony are authorized to try detainees accused of novel war crimes, for example, conspiring to train in a terrorist camp or otherwise provide material assistance to a foreign terrorist organization. Osama bin Laden's driver has been prosecuted by a military commission. Adolph Hitler's chauffer, in contrast, was not tried for war crimes at Nuremberg. Ali al–Bahlul has been prosecuted for making a recruitment video for Al Qaeda abroad that would be constitutionally protected free speech in the United States. According to the United States, feeding Al Qaeda members or teaching them to speak English or to add numbers is a war crime punishable by military commission by facilitating their capabilities to perpetrate terrorism.

Enemy combatants, i.e. persons "associated" in any way with Al Qaeda, are detained indefinitely without accusation or trial. When required to defend its enemy combatant designations in federal courts (even with classified evidence shared only with the judge), the President loses in the overwhelmingly percentage of cases. Non-citizens who have been illegally detained for long years have their detentions routinely extended because the United States refuses them asylum despite their well-founded fears of persecution, torture, or death if returned to their home countries. Chinese Uighurs, detained at Guantanmo Bay for more than eight years before exoneration, were denied asylum despite their legitimate apprehension of torture or execution if deported to China. The United States feared that asylum would provoke China to dump United States debt in retaliation. The American Empire has sold the philosophical soul of the American Republic for a mess of pottage.

Congress passed a law, signed by President Obama, prohibiting the transfer of Guantanmo Bay inmates—whether innocent or not—to the United States on the assumption that all are guilty of terrorism, a version of *Alice in Wonderland's* "sentence first, verdict afterwards."[30] Congress later authorized transfers for the limited purpose of criminal prosecutions in federal civilian courts. If they are acquitted, however, the innocent return to Guantanamo Bay for permanent incarceration as enemy combatants. Heads I win, tails you lose. Orwellian justice.

To circumvent the limited constitutional rights enjoyed by Guantanmo Bay detainees decreed by the United States Supreme Court, some suspected terrorists are incarcerated at Bagram prison in Afghanistan. There, according to the Obama administration, the inmates are outside the law.[31] Bagram is first cousin to the Soviet Union's *Gulag Archipelago* limned by Alexander Solzhenitzen.

The President regularly invokes the state secrets privilege in the American Empire to shield executive branch officials from liability for flagrant violations of constitutional rights, for example, torture, kidnapping, or illegal surveillance. Constitutional rights succumb to national security hysteria. To quote from Marc Antony in Shakespeare's Julius Caesar at a time of political convulsions, "Oh, Judgment thou art fled to brutish beasts, and men have lost their reason."[32]

The American Empire makes secret government the rule and transparency the exception. The people do not know what the executive branch is doing or why in both national security and domestic affairs. Voters knew nothing of the United States torturing Al Qaeda suspects or committing horrific interrogation abuses at Abu Ghraib until the revulsions were leaked to the media. American citizens knew nothing of President George W. Bush's illegal Terrorist Surveillance Program that flouted the criminal prohibitions of the Foreign Intelligence Surveillance Act until the *New York Times'* disclosure in December 2005. President Barack Obama, as authorized by a special congressional statute, has withheld from the public photographs of United States interrogation abuses in a Freedom of Information Act suit filed by the American Civil Liberties Union.

The President and Congress worried that the pictures might spark retaliation against the United States military abroad and compel prosecutions of the American wrongdoers. But if the photos were published and Americans guilty of crimes were punished, respect for the United States and its military abroad would climb, not diminish. The rule of law is universally admired, whereas double standards are universally despised. Publicity and prosecutions would discredit many voices at home and abroad insisting that the United States war on terror is a pretense for a war against Islam - a perception which boosts Al Qaeda's recruitment.

In domestic affairs, even President Obama's *social secretary*, Denise Rogers, is said to be constitutionally immune from testifying before Congress about how White House party crashers evaded detection by the Secret Service during a state dinner on November 24th, 2009. In contrast, the Secret Service provided grand jury testimony about President Clinton-Monica Lewinsky trysts in the 1990s. Ms. Rogers' rebuff to Congressional oversight followed seamlessly from the sneers of President

George Bush's White House political adviser Karl Rove and White House Counsel Harriet Miers at congressional subpoenas to testify about the discharges of nine United States Attorneys. Soon the White House janitor will be placed beyond Congressional scrutiny.

The Executive branch's fetish for secrecy also surfaces in economic affairs. The multi-trillion dollar financial transactions of the Federal Reserve Board in purchasing toxic mortgage-backed securities are secret, and Congress authorizes confidentiality for the 800 billion dollars in bailout payments disbursed under the Troubled Asset Relief Program.

The American Empire's massive secrecy shields public officials from political or legal accountability, the touchstone of government by the consent of the governed celebrated in the Declaration of Independence. John Adams sermonized at the birth of the American Republic:

> [L]iberty cannot be preserved without a general knowledge among the people, who have a right ... to knowledge ... and a desire to know; but besides this, they have a right, an indisputable, unalienable, indefeasible, divine right to that most dreaded and envied kind of knowledge, I mean, of the characters and conduct of their rulers. Rulers are no more than attorneys, agents, and trustees for the people; and if the cause, the interest and trust, is insidiously betrayed, or wantonly trifled away, the people have a right to revoke the authority that they themselves have deputed, and to constitute abler and better agents, attorneys, and trustees...[33]

The American Republic saluted education and transparency as its cornerstones. Freedom and ignorance are incompatible. President George Washington highlighted the centrality of an educated electorate in his first State of the Union Message. Thomas Jefferson elaborated that no nation can be free and ignorant in a state of civilization. James Madison sermonized that knowledge will forever govern ignorance. In addition, the Founding Fathers knew that knowledge in the hands of public officials required transparency to ensure its dedication for the public good, and to avoid its employment to advance private or debased ambitions. Voters must be informed of what the government is doing to guide their political loyalties and activities and to punish wrongdoing through the ballot box. As the historian Henry Steele Commager put it in 1972: "The generation that made the nation thought secrecy in government one of the instruments of Old World tyranny and committed itself to the principle that a democracy cannot function unless the people are permitted to know what their government is up to."[34]

The American Empire has turned the creed of the Republic on its head. The Republic proclaimed that the sole purpose of government is to secure unalienable individual rights to life, liberty, and the pursuit of happiness, i.e. wisdom and virtue. Its philosophy placed the individual at the center of society. It was believed that his liberty was attainable through mere absence of governmental restraints, and that government should be entrusted with few controls and only the mildest supervision over men's affairs. That lofty and revolutionary vision has succumbed to the belief that the mission of the United States is to aggrandize government in the name of national or economic security in a yearning to bequeath risk-free lives to its citizens.

The American Empire's financial extravagance will accelerate its ruination. At present, it is saddled with a national debt exceeding $8 trillion, a $3 trillion budget, and yearly budget deficits surging past $1.5 trillion as far as the eye can see, all to be paid for by posterity. Spiraling spending on Social Security, Medicare, Medicaid, Food Stamps, welfare, and unemployment compensation are unsustainable. Further, the President is empowered to regulate the fine details of the economy at whim, including greenhouse gas emissions, compensation for bank officials, international trade through the World Trade Organization, or compensation to health care providers. Government involvement in the economy during the early years of the Republic, in contrast, was stingy. President Jefferson touted frugality and limited government as the earmarks of enlightened rule:

> [A] wise and frugal Government, which shall restrain men from injuring one another, shall leave them otherwise free to regulate their own pursuits of industry and improvement, and shall not take from the mouth of labor the bread it has earned. This is the sum of good government, and this is necessary to close the circle of our felicities. [35]

Jefferson even urged a constitutional amendment to prohibit government borrowing.

The Founders entrusted the power to regulate interstate or foreign commerce and to spend for the general welfare to Congress, not the President, in furtherance of political accountability. The Supreme Court held in *Clinton v. New York* that Congress was constitutionally forbidden from crowning the President with line-item veto power to arrest its own spending prodigality. The Constitution assigned the power of the purse to Congress with the expectation that it would be brandished to arrest executive usurpations or abuses. James Madison in *Federalist 58* elaborated:

> This power over the purse may, in fact, be regarded as the most complete and effectual weapon with which any constitution can arm the immediate representatives of the people, for obtaining a redress of every grievance, and for carrying into effect every just and salutary measure. [36]

The Republic placed Congress at the apex of the Constitution's hierarchy. It was authorized to demand testimony from every executive official, including the President, to check executive abuses and to inform the people. The Constitution fastened on Congress the non-delegable responsibility for initiating war because it has no incentive to concoct danger, in contrast to the President. Madison underscored the predominance of the legislative branch in *Federalist 48*:

> In a democracy, where a multitude of people exercise in person the legislative functions, and are continually exposed, by their incapacity for regular deliberation and concerted measures, to the ambitious intrigues of their executive magistrates, tyranny may well be apprehended, on some favorable emergency, to start up in the same quarter. But in a representative republic, where the executive magistracy is carefully limited; both in the extent and the duration of its power; and where the legislative power is exercised by an assembly, which is inspired, by a supposed influence over the people, with an intrepid confidence in its own strength; which is sufficiently numerous to feel all the passions which actuate a multitude, yet not so numerous as to be incapable of pursuing the objects of its passions, by means which reason prescribes; it is against the enterprising ambition of this department that the people ought to indulge all their jealousy and exhaust all their precautions. The legislative department derives a superiority in our governments from other circumstances. Its constitutional powers being at once more extensive, and less susceptible of precise limits, it can, with the greater facility, mask, under complicated and indirect measures, the encroachments which it makes

on the co-ordinate departments. It is not unfrequently
a question of real nicety in legislative bodies, whether
the operation of a particular measure will, or will not,
extend beyond the legislative sphere.[37]

In the age of the American Empire, *Federalist 48* is a museum piece.
By elevating party loyalty above institutional prerogatives, Congress has
voluntarily reduced itself to an inkblot on the political landscape.

All muscular powers, including the authority to commence war, have
been ceded to the President as Commander in Chief and as an economic
or environmental Tzar.

The Founding Fathers correctly feared that the President would im-
providently initiate war because military conflict confers on the chief executive patriotic or jingoistic support, secrecy, money, appointments, and
the opportunity for immortality in the history books.

The steady diminution of congressional power has been punctuated
by moments of congressional assertiveness. During the Nixon administration, Congress wielded the power of the purse to end the bombing of Cambodia in 1973 and to prohibit United States ground troops
in Thailand. President Gerald Ford's administration witnessed the so-
called "Church Committee" hearings which disclosed massive civil liberties abuses during 40 years of unchecked spying by the Federal Bureau of
Investigation, Central Intelligence Agency, and National Security Agency.
The Foreign Intelligence Surveillance Act of 1978 and the creation of the
House and Senate Intelligence Committees followed as legislative vehicles
to frustrate an omnipotent President in national security affairs.

But as the American Empire eclipsed the American Republic with the
disintegration of the Soviet Empire in 1991, Congress abandoned completely its already withered role as a check on the executive. Congress
appropriates whatever money the President seeks for war, for economic
stimulus, for health care, etc., as robotically as the Russian Duma follows Prime Minister Vladimir Putin. Legislative drafting now customarily

begins in the White House, not in the branch constitutionally entrusted with legislative power. President Obama deliberated for weeks before announcing on December 1, 2009 the dispatch of 30,000 additional troops to Afghanistan costing tens of billions annually without involving Congress. Not a single Member protested. President Bush similarly stiff-armed Congress in negotiating a new Status of Forces Agreement with Iraq. Congress neglects serious oversight of the wars in Iraq, Afghanistan, and against international terrorism. In contrast, the Fulbright hearings on the Vietnam War beginning in 1966 exposed its flawed assumptions and accelerated its conclusion.

Congress was abjectly subservient to President Bush in passing the Iraq War Resolution endowing him with discretion to commence an invasion. Representative Dick Armey (R. Tex.), then majority leader, on the House floor asked: "Should we vote on this resolution that says, in effect that we, the Congress of the United States, say: 'Mr. President, we trust you and we rely on you in a dangerous time to be our Commander-in-Chief and to use the resources we place at your disposal?' The answer is 'yes.'"[38] Representative Wally Herger (R. Calif.) echoed: "I firmly believe that our President will make the right decision, in the best interests of the United States, and I have the utmost confidence in the integrity of his counsel."[39] Senator Kay Bailey Hutchinson (R. Tex.) urged, "The President has solid information that with a small amount of highly enriched uranium, Iraq could have a nuclear weapon in less than a year."[40] Of course, Iraq had no weapons of mass destruction. It had no mobile biological warfare laboratories. It had no connection with Al Qaeda. It never attempted to purchase yellow cake from Niger. But in the American Empire, the President can do no wrong nor utter any falsehood in fighting under a national security umbrella. Congress is a dependable claque.

It eagerly but unconstitutionally delegated to the President the decision to war with Iraq in the Iraq War Resolution. It was a carbon copy of the ill-starred 1964 Gulf of Tonkin Resolution crowning President Lyndon B. Johnson with discretion to commence war with North Vietnam. But President George Washington, who presided over the Constitutional

Convention of 1787, instructed: "The constitution vests the power of declaring war in Congress; therefore no offensive expedition of importance can be undertaken until after they shall have deliberated upon the subject and authorized such a measure."[41] He was echoed by father of the Constitution, President James Madison, in asking Congress for a declaration of war against Great Britain in 1812.

Yet, the President continues to exercise counter-constitutional authority to initiate preemptive wars to abort pre-embryonic foreign dangers to the United States or its allies. And Congress continues to routinely fund, endorse, or acquiesce in whatever the President ordains as Commander in Chief. A Congressman absurdly declares that the President, like British Kings at the time of the American Revolution, "may deploy military resources at any time without any Congressional approval." Even presidential lies to obtain congressional authorization for war are accepted with equanimity or droopy resignation by Senators and Representatives. The Executive Accountability Act of 2009, which would criminalize intentional presidential deceit to Congress or the American people to obtain authorization for war, meets with congressional yawns and popular indifference.

Abject congressional submissiveness in national security matters is not a partisan issue. Representative Jim Wright (D. Tex.) recalled how he and House Speaker Tip O'Neill (D. Mass.) played supporting actors in foreign affairs to President Ronald Reagan: "He was our President. We owed him that." O'Neil himself had earlier advised: "[W]hen it comes to foreign policy, you support the President."

By cowardly inactivity or passivity, Members become complicit in executive branch crimes like torture or illegal interceptions and retentions of phone conversations or emails. The congressional leadership and key Committee Members remain silent after learning of wrongdoing by the National Security Agency or Central Intelligence Agency. In February 2003, Congresswoman Nancy Pelosi (D. Calif.) learned of illegal waterboarding by the Central Intelligence Agency. Waterboarding constitutes the crime of torture in violation of the federal criminal code by creating an imminent fear of death that provokes prolonged mental trauma. She insisted that she was powerless to do anything about it in a press conference on May 14, 2009. But Pelosi could have disclosed the crime with impunity on the floor of Congress within the Speech or Debate Clause protection announced by the Supreme Court in *Gravel v. United States* (1972). It held that the classified Pentagon Papers could be disclosed by a Senate Committee without fear of reprisal from the executive branch. Pelosi could have introduced legislation prohibiting the expenditure of funds to waterboard detainees; or specifically making waterboarding a crime; or, creating an independent counsel to investigate and prosecute the crime of waterboarding.

But Pelosi choose cowardly silence for partisan political reasons. She wished to avoid making Democrats appear weak on terrorism to the unlearned or uncivilized. She was unmoved by the truism that all that is necessary for the triumph of executive branch evil in the American Empire is for good men and women in Congress to do nothing.

The President's routine assertion of executive privilege to prevent his advisors from complying with congressional subpoenas for testimony does not provoke Congress to retaliate by imposing fines for contempt of Congress or by blocking key presidential appointments. At an earlier stage of Empire, former White House counsel John Dean recited chapter and verse of conversations with then President Richard M. Nixon in the Oval Office to the Senate Watergate Committee. Dean's testimony was pivotal to uncovering Watergate crimes and repudiating the doctrine that if the President does it, it's legal. But with the Empire at its meridian, the contemporary Congress would not protest if Dean were muzzled by the President in comparable circumstances.

The President approves bills passed by Congress, but appends signing statements declaring his intent to ignore provisions that he unilaterally proclaims would unconstitutionally confine his discretion in national security or foreign policy matters or otherwise. Signing statement examples include statutory edicts limiting the President's authority to place United States troops under United Nations command or to meet with nations designated as state sponsors of terrorism. The signing statements are tantamount to absolute line-item vetoes, which the United States Supreme Court held unconstitutional in *Clinton v. NewYork*. They arrogate power over the legislative process to the executive branch by preventing Congress from bundling into one bill provisions the President both likes and dislikes; and, confronting him with the Hobson's choice of either taking the good with the bad or taking nothing. In addition, Congress cannot override a signing statement by two-thirds majorities in the House and Senate because they are unilateral acts of the White House. Congress does nothing to defend its legislative prerogatives, for example, by prohibiting the expenditure of any funds to implement a law to which a signing statement has been appended.

Congressional members perceive themselves as supporting actors in a movie composed and directed by the President. They are disinterested in interrogation abuses, including torture or criminal violations of the Foreign Intelligence Surveillance Act. They largely neglect to ascertain whether monumental bailout spending on irresponsible financial institutions helped or hindered the economy, or whether the secret and vast monetary powers of the Federal Reserve Board have been abused or ill-used. Most Members are only excited about petty preservation of legislative earmarks for favored charities or research institutions. What was said about French King Louis XVI's ill-fated Cabinet might be said of Congress: never to have said anything or done anything is a great power, but ought not to be abused.

During the American Republic, Congress was not so docile. On November 19, 1794, President George Washington reviewed for Congress the Whiskey Rebellion which he had suppressed. He assailed "certain self-created societies," and urged Congress "to turn the machinations of the wicked to the confirming of our constitution: to enable us at all times to root out internal sedition, and put invasion to flight."[42] Congressman William Smith maintained that if the House of Representatives refrained from following President Washington's exhortation, it "would be an avowed desertion of the Executive."[43] But Congressman John Nichols denied that he should "abandon my independence for the sake of the president."[44] Congressman James

Madison, father of the Constitution and Bill of Rights, also balked at submission to President Washington's proposal: "When the people have formed a Constitution, they retain those rights which they have not expressly delegated. It is a question of whether what has been retained can be legislated upon."[45] Madison denied that Congress enjoyed authority to legislate on the liberties of speech or press. He lectured that fidelity to the nature of republican government meant "that the censorial power is in the people over the Government and not in the Government over the people."[46]

When the American Empire began its first steps away from a Republic in the Mexican-American War, then President James K. Polk descried as traitors any who questioned his counterfactual claim that Mexico provoked the conflict by killing American soldiers on American soil.

But for Congressmen Ron Paul (R. Tex), Walter Jones (R. NC), and Dennis Kucinich (D. Ohio), no Member of Congress or national leader has the courage to confront the President with the facts that large American military footprints in Afghanistan and Iraq and wartime assaults on due process and civil liberties are making the nation less safe and less free. The best national defense is a citizenry that loves the country and will be alert without prompting to identify or foil terrorist plots, like the airplane passengers who thwarted Abdulmutallab and Richard Reid.

The Patriot Act's title was embraced to stigmatize critics despite the Act's several constitutionally dubious provisions that were later voided by federal courts. In shepherding the law through Congress, Attorney General John Ashcroft snarled at critics of the Act on December 2, 2001: "[T]o those who scare peace-loving people with phantoms of lost liberty, my message is this: Your tactics only aid terrorists, for they erode our national unity and diminish our resolve. They give ammunition to America's enemies and pause to America's friends."[47] By March of 2010, the United States Solicitor General and former Dean of Harvard Law School was insisting to the United States Supreme Court that a lawyer would be committing a felony by filing legal briefs on behalf of accused terrorist organizations in the same way that Russia and China punish lawyers who defend government detractors.

It was the same in the Third Reich. Reichsmarschall Herman Goering amplified in a 1934 speech:

> Naturally, the common people don't want war but, after all, it is the leaders of a country who determine the policy and it is always a simple matter to drag people along. Whether it is a democracy or a fascist dictatorship or a parliament or a Communist dictatorship, voice or no voice, the people can always be brought to the bidding of the leaders. That is easy. All you have to do is tell them they are being attacked and denounce the pacifists for a lack of patriotism and exposing the country to danger. It works the same in every country.[48]

Associate Justice of the United States Supreme Court and chief United States prosecutor at Nuremberg vividly exposed the danger of suppressing dissent in times of conflict. He elaborated in *West Virginia State Board of Education v. Barnette* (1943) in the middle of World War II:

> Struggles to coerce uniformity of sentiment in support of some end thought essential to their time and country have been waged by many good as well as by evil men. Nationalism is a relatively recent phenomenon but at other times and places the ends have been racial or territorial security, support of a dynasty or regime, and particular plans for saving souls. As first and moderate methods to attain unity have failed, those bent on its accomplishment must resort to an ever-increasing severity. As governmental pressure toward unity becomes

greater, so strife becomes more bitter as to whose unity it shall be... Ultimate futility of such attempts to compel coherence is the lesson of very such effort from the Roman drive to stamp out Christianity as a disturber of its pagan unity, the Inquisition, as a means to religious and dynastic unity, the Siberian exiles as a means to Russian unity, down to the fast failing efforts of our present totalitarian enemies. Those who begin coercive elimination of dissent soon find themselves exterminating dissenters. Compulsory unification of opinion achieves only the unanimity of the graveyard.[49]

Ordinary citizens either cheer or are indifferent to the Empire's war abuses for three main reasons: they are psychically thrilled by the Empire's domination of the planet; its initial primary victims sport names that sound alien, like Hamdan, Hamdi, or Boumediene; and, they are too unschooled in history or philosophy to discern that the Empire will bring ruination to everyone by creating more enemies than are being destroyed. Afghan, Pakistani, and Iraqi civilians are killed by predator drones or indiscriminate bombings. Detainees at Abu Ghraib, Bagram, and in secret dungeons in Central and Eastern Europe have been tortured or otherwise abused. Thomas Paine's *Common Sense* explained how Americans responded in the American Revolutionary War and would respond to comparable brutalities today:

Men of passive tempers look somewhat lightly over the offences of Britain, and, still hoping for the best, are apt to call out, 'Come, come, we shall be friends again, for all this.' But examine the passion and feelings of mankind, Bring the doctrine of reconciliation to the touchstone of nature, and then tell me, whether you can hereafter love, honour, and faithfully serve the power that hath carried fire and sword into your land? If you cannot do all these, then are you only deceiving yourselves, and by your delay bringing ruin upon posterity...But if you say, you can still pass the violations over, then I ask, Hath your house been burnt? Hath your property been destroyed before your face? Are your wife and children destitute of a bed to lie on, or bread to live on? Have you lost a parent or child by their hands, and yourself the ruined and wretched survivor? If you have not, then you are not a judge of those who have. But if you have, and still can shake hands with the murderers, then you are unworthy of the name of husband, father, friend, or lover, and whatever may be your rank or title in life, you have the heart of a coward, and the spirit of a sycophant.[50]

Matthew Alexander wrote about the blow-back effects of torture under a pseudonym in the Outlook Section of *The Washington Post* (November 30, 2008). He had served 14 years in the U.S. Air Force and had begun his career as a Special Operations pilot flying helicopters. He saw combat in Bosnia and Kosovo, became an Air Force counterintelligence agent, and then volunteered to serve in Iraq as a senior interrogator. Mr. Alexander related:

I learned in Iraq that the No. 1 reason foreign fighters flocked there to fight were the abuses carried out at Abu Ghraib and Guantanamo. Our policy of torture was directly recruiting fighters for Al Qaeda in Iraq. The large majority of suicide bombings in Iraq are still carried out by these foreigners. They are also involved in most of the attacks on U.S. and coalition forces in Iraq. It's no exaggeration to say that at least half of our losses and casualties in that country have come at the hands of foreigners who joined the fray because of our program of detainee abuse. The number of U.S. soldiers who have died because of our torture policy will never be definitively known, but it is fair to say that it is close to the number of lives lost on September 11, 2001. How anyone can say that torture keeps Americans safe is beyond me—unless you don't count American soldiers as American.[51]

United States military bases that encroach on foreign sovereignty insult national pride and generate animosity or resentment. That explains why the United States was compelled to remove its air force and naval bases at Clark and Subic Bay, respectively, from the Philippines around 1990. A status of forces agreement compounds the indignity of a foreign military base because it customarily grants United States personnel legal immunity from the jurisdiction of the host nation. Even the populations of closely allied countries like Japan and South Korea resent United States bases because off-base crimes like rape or murder by servicemen are inevitable. In 1995, for example, Okinawa, Japan, erupted in outrage when a 12-year old Okinawan girl was raped by three United States soldiers. Is it any wonder that Okinawans are currently fighting a new United States base there to replace the Futema Marine Air Station?

The media reflects the political culture's infatuation with Empire. Daily news stories, the first drafts of history, aptly report on its exploits yet neglect any evaluation of their nexus to national security. On February 6th, 2009, the *New York Times* reported United States covert assistance to Uganda to launch an attack against one of its rebel groups - the Lord's Resistance Army. The plan failed, scattering fighters who subsequently committed a wave of massacres as they fled. On August 9th, 2009, the same publication reported the new US military perception that climate change is a national security threat. The military worried that floods in countries like Bangladesh could spark humanitarian crises and strife between neighboring states. A United States military response might be required. The report did not question whether flooding in Bangladesh would endanger the United States, although the tsunami in Sri Lanka in 2005 suggested the opposite.[52]

USA Today printed an article on September 30, 2008, entitled "Africans wary of new US Command for continent," that outlined America's decision to create a new military headquarters in Djibouti, called Africom, responsible for all U.S. military operations on the continent.[53] This decision is widely regarded by Africans as an attempt to protect American interests and gain access to natural resources, rather than a counterterrorism gambit.

The *Washington Post* published an article on July 30, 2009, describing President Obama's dispatch of Defense Secretary Robert Gates, Middle East envoy George Mitchell, national security adviser James Jones, and senior aide Dennis Ross to Israel to demand cessation of any further expansion of settlements in the West Bank.[54] Resolving the Palestinian problem may be worthy of a Nobel Peace Prize, but it is marginal at best to the national security of the United States. When Egypt and Jordan signed peace treaties with Israel, America did not become safer. The Israel-Syria dispute over the Golan Heights is untroubling to the security of the United States.

After the 2008 war between Georgia and Russia, the *Wall Street Journal* published an article in September of that year describing a pledge by then Vice-President Dick Cheney of $1 billion in civilian aid to Georgia during his trip to Eastern Europe. The article's author amplified that, "America will help Georgia rebuild and regain its position as one of the world's fastest-growing economies;" and, that, "An important aim of Thursday's stopover and of Mr. Cheney's visits to nearby Azerbaijan and Ukraine this week was to underscore, in light of Russia's newfound assertiveness, the continued U.S. commitment to protecting the young nations that have emerged from the ashes of the old Soviet Union."[55] But why should the United States undertake that task? Belarus has become a virtual Russian satellite without creating a danger to the United States.

AMERICAN EMPIRE: BEFORE THE FALL

These news stories or commentaries never question the premises behind American intervention in foreign countries. They never second-guess why we need to influence nations in Africa, the Middle East, Europe, or elsewhere. They voice no skepticism about the wisdom of American politicians to direct affairs abroad in ways leaders advertise as favorable to national security.

But skepticism is warranted. The United States assisted Islamic radicals in Afghanistan against the Soviet Union, including Osama bin Laden. And then came 9/11. The American Empire's former mujahideen allies are now its mortal enemies, for instance, Gulbudden Hekmatyr. The United States supported Iraq's Saddam Hussein in his war against Iran (1980-1988) before invading Iraq and toppling Saddam as a national security threat. The invasion unwittingly strengthened the radical Islamic regime in Iran with its nuclear ambitions, state sponsorship of terrorism, and support for Hezbollah and Hamas. Earlier, in 1953, the United States overthrew Iran's democratic Prime Minister Mohammad Mossedegh in favor of the effete and corrupt Shah. The coup culminated a quarter century later in the Iranian revolution and the ascendancy of United States' arch-enemy Ayatollah Khomeini. The United States orchestrated the coup against President Jacobo Arbenz in Guatamala in favor of a series of repressive military regimes. A variation of Guatamala was the United States sponsored overthrow of Chilean President Salvador Allende by General Augustino Pinochet. His dictatorship featured torture, extrajudicial killings, and even the terrorist killings of Orlando Letelier and Ronnie Moffitt in the United States. But United States National Security Advisor and Secretary of State Henry Kissinger defended the U.S. intervention: "I don't see why we need to stand by and watch a country go communist due to the irresponsibility of its people...."[56]

The benevolence and constitutionality of the American Empire are treated by both citizens and political leaders as non-debatable facts like Newton's Laws of Motion. Voices against the Empire's profanation of the nation's signature creed in undertaking perpetual and global warfare are virtually inaudible.

EMPIRE WITHOUT A CAUSE

The American Empire honors beauty more than brains, professional sports more than learning, and power more than philosophical wisdom or courage. Never in the history of the United States have so many known so little about so much.

Truths about the American Empire's adolescent culture and ambitions are unflattering. Prospects for regaining the American Republic are dim. What is necessary is a political culture that prefers freedom to a quest for a risk-free existence and global domination. As Edmund Burke remarked:

> Men are qualified for civil liberty, in exact proportion to their disposition to put moral chains upon their own appetites; in proportion as their love of justice is above their rapacity; in proportion as their soundness and sobriety of understanding is above their vanity and presumption; in proportion as they are more disposed to listen to the counsels of the wise and good, in preference to the flattery of knaves. Society cannot exist unless a controlling power upon will and appetite be placed somewhere and the less of it there is within, the more there must be without. . . men of intemperate minds cannot be free. Their passions forge their fetters.[57]

In other words, as Pogo would have remarked, we have met the enemy of the Republic, and we are they.

The American Republic will be at hand when every American soldier stationed abroad is returned to the United States by congressional edict and universal conscription to defend only the United States on American soil is restored. It will be revived when every United States Treaty or

Executive Agreement obligating Americans to fight and die for others is revoked by the President or overridden by congressional statute. It will flourish when every American voter insists on the impeachments and removals from office of every President, Cabinet member, or Member of Congress who flouts the Constitution. It will thrive when unilateral presidential wars are criminalized. And it will reach its zenith when the exclusive mission of the United States government is to secure to Americans unalienable rights to life, liberty, and the pursuit of happiness. That miraculous transformation, however, would defy the precedents of every previous Empire.

2

How Far The Republic Has Fallen – From Lexington And Concord To The Korangal Valley

The nineteenth of April, 1775, was the rosy-fingered dawn of the American Republic. For the first time, American "Minutemen" spilled their blood in open hostilities with the British Redcoats at Lexington and Concord, twin cities immortalized in William Henry Longfellow's *Midnight Ride of Paul Revere.* 58

The Minutemen were not professional soldiers. They were ordinary men with uncommon courage and convictions about freedom and sovereignty. At Lexington, eight gave that last full measure of devotion to establish a Republic. Their names are engraved on the Battle Monument in Lexington Green: Ensign Robert Munroe, Jonas Parker, Samuel Hadley, Jonathan Harrington, Jr., Isaac Muzzey, Caleb Harrington, John Brown, and Asahel Porter. They died fighting on American soil to secure liberty for themselves and their posterity, not to establish an Empire to dominate others through endless global war. To them, the law was king, the king was not law, as Thomas Paine wrote in *Common Sense.* 59

Travel a short distance from Lexington to gaze at the Concord Minuteman, sculpted in 1874 by Daniel Chester. It testifies to the common citizen's devotion to freedom and fierce revulsion of tyranny at the nation's birth. The transfixing statue is complemented by Ralph Waldo Emerson's *Concord Hymn,* composed in 1836 before the United States began to trade its safe Republic for an unsafe Empire under the mindless banner of Manifest Destiny in the 1846-1848 Mexican-American War:

> By the rude bridge that arched the flood,
> Their flag to April's breeze unfurled,
> Here once the embattled farmers stood,
> And fired the shot heard round the world,
> The foe long since in silence slept,
> Alike the Conqueror silent sleeps,
> And Time the ruined bridge has swept
> Down the dark stream which seaward creeps.
>
> On this green bank, by this soft stream,
> We set to-day a votive stone,
> That memory may their deed redeem,
> When like our sires our sons are gone.
> Spirit! who made those freemen dare
> To die, or leave their children free,
> Bid time and nature gently spare
> The shaft we raise to them and Thee.[60]

The embattled farmers fought for ideas that later found expression in the nation's Charter Documents: the Declaration of Independence, the United States Constitution, George Washington's Farewell Address, and John Quincy Adams' July 4, 1821 oration. They expounded the nation's revolutionary philosophy: individual liberty and due process over a national security state; government by the consent of the governed; a separation of powers; checks and balances; and sovereignty in "We the

People," not in a King or monarch. The Charter Documents insisted that the purpose of government is exhausted by securing unalienable rights to life, liberty, and the pursuit of happiness *to ourselves and our posterity*.[61] The Constitution stipulated that federal government authority was confined to subjects expressly enumerated or reasonably implied. The slogan that government is more the problem than the solution is not a modern invention. It was the insight of James Madison in the *Federalist Papers:*

> If angels were to govern men, neither external nor internal controls on government would be necessary. In framing a government which is to be administered by men over men, the great difficulty lies in this: you must first enable the government to control the governed; and in the next place oblige it to control itself. A dependence on the people is, no doubt, the primary control on the government; but experience has taught mankind the necessity of auxiliary precautions.[62]

Also authored by Madison, the Bill of Rights attempts to arrest government power. The First Amendment, for example, prohibits government from infringing on freedom of speech, press, religion, and the right to petition for redress of grievances. It additionally blocks government from sponsoring religion. The Second Amendment prohibits government from infringing on the right to keep and bear arms. The Fourth Amendment forbids unreasonable police searches or seizures and celebrates a right to be left alone. The Fifth Amendment proscribes government takings of property without just compensation. It further condemns deprivations of life, liberty, or property without due process of law or compulsory self-incrimination. The Sixth Amendment prevents government overreaching in criminal prosecutions. It establishes a right to a jury of peers; a right to counsel; a right to confront accusers; a right to call defense witnesses; and, a prohibition on successive prosecutions for the same offense. The Eighth Amendment bans cruel and unusual punishments. The Bill of Rights is emphatically *not* a prescription for government regulation, welfare programs, bailouts of private enterprise, or otherwise. Indeed, the Constitution eschews imposing on government any affirmative obligations whatsoever, except to pay for private property taken by eminent domain.

As for prosperity, the Founding Fathers were guided by the wisdom of Scottish economist Adam Smith writing in 1776:

> Little else is required to carry a state to the highest degree of affluence from the lowest barbarism but peace, easy taxes, and a tolerable administration of justice; all the rest being brought about by the natural course of things. All governments which thwart this natural course, which force things into another channel, or which endeavor to arrest the progress of society at a particular point, are unnatural, and, to support themselves, are obliged to be oppressive and tyrannical.[63]

The Constitution, before the Sixteenth Amendment in 1914, denied Congress authority to levy an income tax. The revenues of the federal government were modest, derived largely from tariffs and excise taxes. In 1912, federal revenues were $921 million, and the corresponding budget deficit was $3.5 million.

The American Republic renounced Empire in the Constitution's Preamble. It conspicuously excluded utopian schemes to save the world from tyranny or humanitarian horrors. It cherished above all else a more perfect union featuring the blessings of liberty to Americans, period, with no question marks, commas, or semicolons.

HOW FAR THE REPUBLIC HAS FALLEN

The Lexington and Concord Minutemen risked their lives to defeat concentrated executive power. The British monarch was empowered unilaterally to initiate war and to sacrifice the lives of British subjects to win personal fame, glory, aggrandizement, or to avenge personal insults. In the half-century before April 1775, the Founding Fathers witnessed chronic European conflicts for conquest and domination irrelevant to the preservation of national sovereignty, including the French and Indian War of 1757-63 in which American colonists fought for the British King. Future Chief Justice John Jay elaborated in *The Federalist Papers*: "absolute monarchs will often make war when their nations are to get nothing by it, but for purposes and objects merely personal, such as a thirst for military glory, revenge for personal affronts, ambition, or private compacts to aggrandize or support their particular families or partisans."[64] Those and other motives, "which affect only the mind of the sovereign, often lead him to engage in wars not sanctified by justice or by the voice and interests of his people."[65]

The Minutemen at Lexington fought for an American Republic featuring three cardinal creeds. First, America's influence abroad would be limited to the force of example, meaning that it would desist from nation building. It would reject wars to liberate oppressed peoples elsewhere with no loyalty to America or subjection to American laws. In addition, the Republic would disavow any moral obligation to spread freedom or democracy across the globe. The Minutemen anticipated then Secretary of State John Quincy Adams' July 4, 1821 address:

> [The United States] has, in the lapse of nearly half a century, without a single exception, respected the independence of other nations, while asserting and maintaining her own. She has abstained from interference in the concerns of others, when the conflict has been for principles to which she clings, as to the last vital drop that visits the heart...She is the well-wisher to the freedom and independence of all.

> She is the champion and vindicator only of her own... She
> might become the dictatress of the world: she would be
> no longer the ruler of her own spirit."[66]

The Secretary of State had heeded the admonition of British states-man Edmund Burke that the British Empire itself had ignored: "I dread our own power and our own ambition. I dread our being too much dread-ed. It is ridiculous to say that we are not men, and that, as men, we shall never wish to aggrandize ourselves."[67]

Second, the United States would practice the political maxims en-shrined in the Declaration of Independence and Constitution: that all men are created equal; that they are endowed with unalienable rights to life, liberty, and the pursuit of happiness (i.e., wisdom and virtue); that gov-ernments are established to secure these rights, deriving their just powers from the consent of the governed; that due process of law is the great-est safeguard ever discovered for the preservation of liberty; and, that freedom and transparency should be rules and government coercion and secrecy exceptions in the Republic's political domain.

Third, the Republic could preserve liberty and self-government and avoid a return to a monarch-like Empire only if the living were willing to sacrifice for posterity, for example, by keeping undefiled the institu-tions and precedents of a Republic that make the individual the center of society and repudiate government aggrandizements. That requires resist-ing every encroachment on liberty or sacrilege to the rule of law at their inceptions. James Madison admonished:

> It is proper to take alarm at the first experiment on
> our liberties. We hold this prudent jealousy to be the
> first duty of citizens and one of the noblest character-
> istics of the late Revolution. The freemen of America
> did not wait till usurped power had strengthened itself

by exercise and entangled the question in precedents.
They saw all the consequences in the principle, and they
avoided the consequences by denying the principle. We
revere this lesson too much ... to forget it.[68]

The Republic's principles for which the Minutemen died are routinely ignored. The United States has become an Empire featuring precedents that sanction government lawlessness and unchecked power in the name of national security or economic well being. The commanding heights of authority have been voluntarily surrendered by Congress and the American people to the President. Secrecy, not government by the consent of the governed, has become the norm. Individual liberty—freedom from arbitrary detention or torture and the right to be left alone—is readily subordinated to the flimsiest claims of danger. The mission of the United States is no longer individual freedom safeguarded by sharp limits on government power. It has degenerated into world control or domination achieved by crowning the President with unlimited authority to deploy the military and impose martial law everywhere on the globe in perpetuity, to trample individual liberties, and to make the people financially dependent on government.

The death of the American Republic at the hands of the American Empire can be vividly demonstrated by comparing the Minutemen with the Second Platoon of Company B of the First Battalion, 26th Infantry, in Afghanistan on Wednesday, April 15th, 2009, as reported in *The New York Times*.[69] The comparison date is 234 years after the immortalized deaths and courage of the Minutemen at Lexington and Concord, and approximately three months after the inauguration of President Barack Obama.

Hurled into a perpetual and global "war" against international terrorism, the Second Platoon departed its base in Afghanistan's Korangal Valley, thousands of miles away from American shores, on a mission to speak with local elders in the village of Laneyal. It hoped to ascertain whether they support or oppose the U.S. military presence attempting to subdue the valley. That was a fool's errand, because the answer depended on whether the United States would remain in Afghanistan as long as necessary to protect the elders from retaliation by Taliban or Al Qaeda and whether the United States would coerce President Hamid Karzai to operate an efficient, non-corrupt government that commanded popular loyalty. The platoon could not have answered either question.

The Korangalis—an isolated Afghan people with a language unrelated to Pashto or Dari, the two main Afghan tongues—had engaged the American Army in a bloody standoff over a small piece of territory for three years. Yet, the hapless Afghanis were not contemplating a war of aggression against the United States. Prior to the arrival of American troops in the Korangal Valley, the Korangalis had little association with the Taliban and the valley was not a major haven for insurgents or Al Qaeda. As Lt. Col. Brian Pearl, who oversees U.S. military operations in the Korangal valley, elaborated, "I don't believe there are any hard-core Taliban in the valley."[70] Major James Fussell, a former Army Special Forces soldier who fought in the valley, echoed Lt. Col. Pearl's statement: "Occasionally a Taliban or Al Qaeda member was transiting through that location, but the Korangalis were by no means part of the insurgency. Unfortunately, now they are because they were willing to accept any help to get us out."[71]

As is customary in insurgencies, the Korangalis fought for various motives. Some supported the Taliban because of their shared camaraderie with fighters for a radical Islam. Some feared Taliban reprisals. Some aimed to kill U.S. and coalition soldiers because they resented the corrupt and inept American puppet government of President Karzai. He had banned virtually all timber cutting and thus crippled the local logging industry. The timber dispute found expression in the platoon's Korangal outpost itself. It occupied a former sawmill whose displaced owner, Hajji Matin, had become a leader of the local insurgency. Matin's embrace of the Taliban occurred only after the Afghan government banned timber trade, thus depriving him of his sole means of income, and followed the deaths of several family members killed by a U.S. airstrike.[72] Underlining all of these motivations was the population's cultural enmity towards outsiders, entrenched through a long history of resistance against foreign incursions. If the United States military were not present in Afghanistan, the Korangalis would never have taken up hostilities against Americans. *Not a single one was plotting to attack the United States. The overwhelming majority simply desired to be left alone.*

The Second Platoon reached Aliabad, the village on the slope opposite Laneyal, and began the descent down a stone staircase to the river. With several soldiers remaining in Aliabad with guns aimed at the opposite side, two squads and the officers crossed a narrow footbridge and reached a point where two branches of the river converge. The lead squad crossed the second bridge, entering a terraced wheat field, while the Taliban waited patiently.

As the first six Americans began walking along the opposite side of the river, the Taliban struck, detonating a massive explosion next to the men. A plume of dirt and rock shot into the air, signaling the insurgents to begin their assault. U.S. soldiers dashed from the kill zone as they came under intense small-arms fire, frantically attempting to respond in kind. As the firefight progressed, American aircraft and artillery pounded the suspected insurgent positions, destroying various village buildings in the area. As the battle shifted in favor of the Americans, the Taliban melted away. The U.S soldiers could only guess if any had been killed or wounded.

The Platoon soon realized that one of their men—Private Richard "Rick" Dewater—was missing. A search party of American and Afghan forces was immediately dispatched. Hours after the ambush, the soldiers found Private Dewater's body suspended from a tree. He had been killed by the initial Taliban explosion. A helicopter arrived at the Korangal outpost during the night to retrieve Dewater's corpse and started his long journey home. Engulfed in a flag-draped coffin, he was reunited with his family days later at his funeral in Roseburg, Oregon—another victim of the mindless American Empire. With congressional acquiescence, the President prohibited news photos of the returning coffin to conceal the realities of war.

AMERICAN EMPIRE: BEFORE THE FALL

Private Dewater did not die on American soil in defense of American lives or liberties like the martyrs at Lexington. The threat to the United States from Afghani insurgents was trivial in comparison to the British Redcoats who represented an Empire that ruled the seas and realistically aimed to reduce American colonists to semi-vassalage. The raw military power of Great Britain dwarfed that of General George Washington's Continental Army, whereas Taliban was to the American armed forces what an acorn is to a mighty oak. Defeat in the Revolutionary War would have meant execution of the Founding Fathers as traitors. They pledged their lives, their fortunes, and their sacred honor in the Declaration of Independence in dissolving America's ties to Great Britain. In contrast, Dewater was conducting offensive warfare, not defending against an Afghan attack on the United States.

The threat posed by the Taliban and Al Qaeda to United States sovereignty is trivial. In October 2007, the *New York Times* reported that the Taliban might field as many as ten thousand fighters, but a much smaller fraction—less than three thousand—were full-time insurgents. The number of Al Qaeda in Afghanistan is a microscopic 100 (as of December 2009), and in neighboring Pakistan Al Qaeda is only modestly less invisible.[73] The combined threat of each group is but a shadow of the Soviet Red Army or the German Wehrmacht. Neither is endowed with government power to tax or to conscript. They have no scientists to develop advanced weapons. They have no economic wherewithal to sustain continuous active warfare. Their capacity or inclination to traverse thousands of miles to cause mayhem in the United States falls far short of the constitutional threshold for war—less than the risk of another Timothy McVeigh or plots to kill high-level officials with anthrax.

United States citizens at home are vastly less likely to be killed by Taliban or Al Qaeda than by a domestic murderer. Three thousand Americans have been killed by international terrorists in the United States during and since September 11th, 2001. In that same interval, approximately 153,000 murders have been perpetrated in the United States, and only 61% of the criminal homicides result in a suspect's arrest, let alone a conviction.[74] Claims that Al Qaeda threatens to install a Caliphate in Washington, D.C. emerge from fevered imaginations that exploit popular fear of Islam. The claims are given credence because the psychology of Empire magnifies danger to justify a national security state. Jihadists, unlike domestic murderers, may covet the overthrow of the United States government in favor of an Islamic theocracy. But a malicious intent with no accomplishment potential does not pass the demarcation line between a criminal act and an act of war.

Contrary to President Obama, Afghanistan is a war of choice, not a war of necessity. That explains why he has set a 2011 semi-deadline to begin withdrawing American forces there. He knows the troops thousands of miles away from American shores are unnecessary to preventing another 9/11.

Besides the obvious grief felt by his friends and family, Private Dewater's killing passed virtually unnoticed by the American public. No *Concord Hymn, Paul Revere's Ride,* or *Gettysburg Address* was composed to memorialize his death. His sacrifice inspired neither reverence nor oblations. He did not die for a government of the people, by the people, for the people. His death did not make the United States safer, freer, or more prosperous. He died senselessly for an Empire endlessly at war everywhere on the planet to enjoy the juvenile thrill of domination and swagger. The United States has come full circle from fighting an Empire to becoming an Empire.

On June 25, 2009, the same day as Michael Jackson's death, Lt. Brian Bradshaw was killed in Afghanistan by an explosive device. His niece, Martha Gillis of Springfield, Virginia, wrote in a letter to the editor of *The Washington Post,* published on July 5, 2009: "Where was the coverage of my nephew or the other soldiers who died that week?...What more... did Michael Jackson do or represent that earned him memorial 'shrines,' while this soldier's death goes unheralded?"[75] The American people are largely indifferent to the wars in Iraq and Afghanistan and international terrorism because they viscerally know the conflicts are extraneous to their security. Moreover, the all-volunteer armed forces are numerically dominated by the voiceless and powerless.

In 1970, Vietnam veteran and future Democratic presidential nominee John Kerry spoke about senseless American deaths in the Vietnam War:

> Now we are told that the men who fought there must watch quietly while American lives are lost so that we can exercise the incredible arrogance of Vietnamizing the Vietnamese... Each day to facilitate the process by which the United States washes her hands of Vietnam someone has to give up his life so that the United States doesn't have to admit something that the entire world already knows, so that we can't say we have made a mistake...Someone has to die so that President Nixon won't be, and these are his words, 'the first President to lose a war.' We are asking Americans to think about that, because how do you ask a man to be the last man to die in Vietnam? How do you ask a man to be the last man to die for a mistake?[76]

Today, Senator John Kerry (D. Mass.), chairman of the Senate Foreign Relations Committee, has forgotten his own words in asking American men and women to die fighting in Afghanistan so that the Democratic Party can say it is tough on terrorism and national security issues. The more things change, the more they stay the same. If John Quincy Adams' July 4 address had been mastered and followed by President Obama, Private Dewater would still be alive, and the United States would be safer from external attack.

Dewater and his Second Platoon fought for causes and held beliefs repudiated by the American Republic. They were probably convinced that they should decamp to Afghanistan to advance democracy and human rights there just as British soldiers at the apogee of the British Empire believed in their professed civilizing missions to South Africa, Afghanistan, India, Burma, Nigeria, and otherwise. Dewater died seeking to secure liberty for Afghans who owed no allegiance to the United States and who had done nothing to benefit America. In contrast, the Minutemen fought only for Americans. They did not seek to liberate other subjects of the British Empire—even Canadians.

That is not to say the Founding Fathers would have deplored American volunteers who might assist in the liberation of foreigners from subjugation. Indeed, they deeply appreciated and commemorated the military services of the Frenchman Marquis De Lafayette and Pole Casimir Pulaski. But they distinguished sharply between citizens *ordered* by their government to risk life and limb for foreign peoples, on the one hand, and altruism on the other hand. The Charter Documents, as previously noted, largely celebrate *restraints* on government because of their deep-rooted skepticism of government motives and wisdom.

The Founding Fathers knew what was unknowable. They recognized that the knowledge required to transform longstanding despotisms or tribal cultures like Afghanistan's into democracies was beyond the human ken. Of all the sciences, political science is the most stunted. The American Empire, in contrast, believes nothing is impossible in nation-building, a conviction akin to believing in a perpetual motion machine but with more frightful consequences. Mistakes are callously acknowledged, but only after catastrophic consequences. Approximately one year after Dewater's death, American forces closed down the Korangal outpost on April 14th, 2010, and removed all forces from the valley. Their withdrawal testified to the purposeless attempt to dominant the valley purportedly to aid its inhabitants. According the *New York Times,* the fighting in the region "did more to spawn insurgents than defeat them."[77] Ignorance and arrogance were in the saddle. Reflecting on his time battling insurgents in the valley, Major Fussell observed:

> The whole point of counterinsurgency is that by secur-
> ing the local population, you legitimize the govern-
> ment of Afghanistan. But the thing about the Korangal
> and Waygal Vallyes is that they don't recognize any gov-
> ernment beyond their little village and when you go
> to them and say, 'we want to secure you and offer you
> a road' they say, 'we don't want a road.' I would argue
> you couldn't find a single Korangali who wanted any
> outside assistance.[78]

He added, "We had the best intentions, but when you don't fully understand the culture" it is impossible to make the right choices.[79] In a small pocket of the Afghan war, Private Dewater and 41 other coura-geous soldiers lost their lives for the juvenile thrill of national swagger or chestiness.

Dewater and his fallen comrades died for an Empire whose prac-tices more resemble the monarchy of King George III than the American Republic: unlimited war making power in the president; military com-missions in lieu of civilian courts; denial of habeas corpus; global war with the aim of eliminating even miniscule foreign dangers to the United States; detentions without accusation or trial; state secrets to protect constitutional wrongdoers; illegal spying; presidential signing statements; torture and sister interrogation abuses; extraordinary rendition to third countries practicing torture; and mutilating the rule of law by shield-ing high level government officials from criminal prosecution for felo-nies, like torture or warrantless interceptions of emails or phone calls of Americans on American soil in contravention of the Foreign Intelligence Surveillance Act.

The primary culprits in the death of the American Republic, the tri-umph of the American Empire, and the tragedy of Private Dewater's death are the American people. The United States Constitution recognizes "We the People" as sovereign. Politics and policy in the United States reflect public opinion. Citizens are not clamoring to restore the practices and principles of the American Republic celebrated by the Founding Fathers, including limited government, due process, the right to be left alone, and an end to every ongoing foreign military intervention, treaty commitment, or base. If the American people had rejected Empire with their votes, no elected leader would have continued down that path. But Americans have become indifferent to their freedoms and the thrill and responsibilities of self-government. They have justified Fyodor Dostoyevsky's lament in The Grand Inquisitor chapter of *The Brothers Karamozov* that human beings will eagerly trade their freedom for food and security.

This citizen plunge to vassalage or serfdom to an omnipotent presidency featuring a national security state can be appreciated only by examining the American Republic at its birth informed by the genius of the Founding Fathers. As Cicero taught, "Freedom is participation in power."[80]

3

The Nation's Charter Documents

The Founding Fathers enshrined their unsurpassed prescience and understanding of human nature in four Charter Documents: the Declaration of Independence, the United States Constitution, President George Washington's Farewell Address, and then Secretary of State John Quincy Adams' July 4, 1821 address. Collectively they are the political philosophy of the American Republic. They recognize that the exclusive purpose of the United States is to secure the blessings of liberty to ourselves and our posterity through strict adherence to the rule of law and a separation of powers; and, that the United States was not created to build an empire or to control or dominate others by military force or threats. That latter endeavor would defeat the purpose of the American Republic by concentrating unchecked power and secrecy in a monarch-like President, as John Quincy Adams explained in his July 4 address. Finally, these Charter Documents—specifically the Farewell Address—championed American neutrality towards all nations and renunciation of preemptive warfare.

President Washington's Farewell Address teaches that the United States should eschew political entanglements while building defenses sufficient to deter foreign attacks. Not a syllable indicates that Washington would have transformed the Republic into a global military behemoth despite changes in the international landscape and the vast geographical expansion of the United States across the Continent and beyond. He preached precepts that would be disparaged as "isolationism" by today's champions of the American Empire:

> The great rule of conduct for us in regard to foreign nations is in extending our commercial relations, to have with them as little political connection as possible. So far as we have already formed engagements, let them be fulfilled with perfect good faith. Here let us stop. Europe has a set of primary interests which to us have none; or a very remote relation. Hence she must be engaged in frequent controversies, the causes of which are essentially foreign to our concerns. Hence, therefore, it must be unwise in us to implicate ourselves by artificial ties in the ordinary vicissitudes of her politics, or the ordinary combinations and collisions of her friendships or enmities.[81]

Washington conspicuously omitted insinuating that the United States should employ military force to overthrow despotisms and seek to give birth to democracies because the latter would be less likely to initiate war against the United States than would tyrannies or empires. He remembered that the Revolutionary War was fought against the most democratic nation in the world. He further understood the moral and pragmatic imperative of standing aloof from foreign controversies that do not impact United States sovereignty. He did not perceive the rise of Napoleon's Empire as any greater danger to the United States than France's less dictatorial predecessor government.

Washington regarded protecting the nation's neutrality in any conflict and deterring foreign attacks through invincible defenses at home as the alpha and omega of the American military policy (although he accepts the possibility that a choice for war might be appropriate in some circumstances). He nowhere hints that the United States should commence wars thousands of miles from the nation's shores to prevent remote threats from ripening into authentic dangers. He rejected the heresy that the best defense is a good offense. He never contemplated the preemptive war doctrine of the American Empire:

> Our detached and distant situation invites and enables us to pursue a different course. If we remain one people under an efficient government, the period is not far off when we may defy material injury from external annoyance; when we may take such an attitude as will cause the neutrality we may at any time resolve upon to be scrupulously respected; when belligerent nations, under the impossibility of making acquisitions upon us, will not lightly hazard the giving us provocation; when we may choose peace or war, as our interest, guided by justice, shall counsel.

> Why forego the advantages of so peculiar a situation? Why quit our own to stand upon foreign ground? Why, by interweaving our destiny with that of any part of Europe, entangle our peace and prosperity in the toils of European ambition, rivalship, interest, humor or caprice?

> It is our true policy to steer clear of permanent alliances with any portion of the foreign world; so far, I mean, as we are now at liberty to do it; for let me not be understood as capable of patronizing infidelity to

existing engagements. I hold the maxim no less applicable to public than to private affairs, that honesty is always the best policy. I repeat it, therefore, let those engagements be observed in their genuine sense. But, in my opinion, it is unnecessary and would be unwise to extend them.[82]

Washington shunned new military alliances of any sort. During his presidency, the United States inked no defense treaties like NATO. It remained neutral in the war between Great Britain and France. He, like the other Founding Fathers, feared that military alliances would corrupt the Republic's philosophical soul. They knew that the typical foreign leader would have had no qualms dining with Jesus at The Last Supper and breakfasting the next morning with Pontius Pilate.

As regards foreign economic intercourse, President Washington was adamant against scheming by military force or otherwise to obtain special favors or access to ostensible strategic commodities. Neutrality or evenhandedness was again his watchword:

> Harmony, liberal intercourse with all nations, are recommended by policy, humanity, and interest. But even our commercial policy should hold an equal and impartial hand; neither seeking nor granting exclusive favors or preferences; consulting the natural course of things; diffusing and diversifying by gentle means the streams of commerce, but forcing nothing; establishing (with powers so disposed, in order to give trade a stable course, to define the rights of our merchants, and to enable the government to support them) conventional rules of intercourse, the best that present circumstances and mutual opinion will permit, but

temporary, and liable to be from time to time abandoned or varied, as experience and circumstances shall dictate; constantly keeping in view that it is folly in one nation to look for disinterested favors from another; that it must pay with a portion of its independence for whatever it may accept under that character; that, by such acceptance, it may place itself in the condition of having given equivalents for nominal favors, and yet of being reproached with ingratitude for not giving more. There can be no greater error than to expect or calculate upon real favors from nation to nation. It is an illusion, which experience must cure, which a just pride ought to discard.[83]

Washington at no point insinuates that the United States should resort to military force to secure access to allegedly strategic materials to bolster the nation's economy, or to compel foreign nations to embrace free trade as opposed to mercantilism to boost economic growth.

The Charter Documents recognize that a healthy economy does not require a global military footprint to forestall conceivable embargos or export controls from curtailing supplies of key resources or to prevent disruption of trading patterns caused by foreign wars. From 1776 to 1846, the United States economy flourished without the establishment of a single American military base on foreign soil. From the Presidency of Washington in 1789 to the Presidency of James K. Polk in 1844, the United States economy grew at a rapid rate along with foreign trade. Foreign wars did not stifle economic expansion. Nor was the United States deprived of a single important resource. Smuggling or bribery or middlemen invariably sabotage efforts to deprive any country of an ostensible critical resource or arms. During the Napoleonic Wars from 1794-1815, and the Central and South American revolt against Spain and Portugal from 1810-1829, the United States economy galloped. It was not denied access to essential commodities. It was not excluded from foreign trade by the absence of military deployments outside the United States.

Then Secretary of State John Quincy Adams brilliantly summarized the Republic's undeviating adherence to the philosophy elaborated in Washington's Farewell Address, the Declaration of Independence, and the Constitution, in his July 4, 1821 address. Chronicling the international accomplishments of the United States through example, Adams ardently defended the nation's adamant refusal to employ force to extend liberty to persons with no allegiance to the United States:

[W]hat has America done for the benefit of mankind?

Let our answer be this: America, with the same voice which spoke herself into existence as a nation, proclaimed to mankind the inextinguishable rights of human nature, and the only lawful foundations of government. America, in the assembly of nations, since her admission among them, has invariably, though often fruitlessly, held forth to them the hand of honest friendship, of equal freedom, of generous reciprocity.

She has uniformly spoken among them, though often to heedless and often to disdainful ears, the language of equal liberty, of equal justice, and of equal rights.

She has, in the lapse of nearly half a century, without a single exception, respected the independence of other nations while asserting and maintaining her own.

She has abstained from interference in the concerns of others, even when conflict has been for principles to which she clings, as to the last vital drop that visits the heart.

She has seen that probably for centuries to come, all the contests of that Aceldama the European world, will be contests of inveterate power, and emerging right.

Wherever the standard of freedom and Independence has been or shall be unfurled, there will her heart, her benedictions and her prayers be.

But she goes not abroad, in search of monsters to destroy.

She is the well-wisher to the freedom and independence of all.

She is the champion and vindicator only of her own.

She will commend the general cause by the countenance of her voice, and the benignant sympathy of her example.

She well knows that by once enlisting under other banners than her own, were they even the banners of foreign independence, she would involve herself beyond the power of extrication, in all the wars of interest and intrigue, of individual avarice, envy, and ambition, which assume the colors and usurp the standard of freedom.

The fundamental maxims of her policy would insensibly change from liberty to force. The frontlet upon her brows would no longer beam with the ineffable splendor of freedom and independence; but in its stead would soon be substituted an imperial diadem, flashing in false and tarnished luster the murky radiance of dominion and power.

She might become the dictatress of the world. She would be no longer the ruler of her own spirit....

[America's] glory is not dominion, but liberty. Her march is the march of the mind. She has a spear and a shield: but the motto upon her shield is, Freedom, Independence, Peace. This has been her Declaration: this has been, as far as her necessary intercourse with the rest of mankind would permit, her practice.[84]

From independence until the Mexican-American War of 1846, the United States honored its Charter Documents. During this Golden Age of the Republic, America never contemplated or yearned for a military force capable of overthrowing the Ottoman Empire, the French Bourbons, the Ming Dynasty, the Russian Romanovs, or any other tyrannical regime. The United States did not fight on behalf of the Greeks in their War of

Independence from the Ottoman Empire commencing in 1821. It offered no military assistance to Central or South America in revolt against their colonial oppressors—Spain and Portugal. The Republic played spectator to foreign injustices and helotry despite the Declaration of Independence recognizing the universal duty of oppressed people to revolt against tyranny. The Republic offered only its example and sympathies.

Liberty stands at the apex of the Constitution. But the Founding Fathers knew with a certainty that the liberties of American citizens would be crippled by any attempt to spread freedom abroad through military force. That mission would concentrate all power in the President and subordinate every liberty to national security clamors. Cicero taught that, "In time of war, the law falls silent."[85] War makes legal what is customarily murder. Habeas corpus can be suspended. Secrecy regularly trumps transparency. Freedom of speech, press, association and due process are routinely violated.

Madison saw firsthand how the nation's undeclared war with France in 1798 gave birth to the ill-conceived Alien and Sedition Acts—passed by Congress with a Federalist Party majority and signed into law by President John Adams. The Sedition Act criminalized criticism of the President or Congress in flagrant violation of the First Amendment (while cynically excluding verbal assaults on Vice President Thomas Jefferson, a Democrat-Republican). The Sedition Act punished any person who:

> shall write, print, utter, or publish, or shall cause or procure to be written, printed, uttered, or published, or shall knowingly and willingly assist or aid in writing, printing, uttering, or publishing any false, scandalous and malicious writing or writings against the government of the United States, or either House of the Congress of the United States, or the President of the United States, with intent to defame the said government, or either House of the said Congress, or the said

> President, or to bring them, or either of them, into
> contempt or disrepute; or to excite against them, or
> either or any of them, the hatred of the good people of
> the United States....[86]

Under this statute, 25 men, primarily editors of the opposition party's (Democratic-Republican) newspapers, were arrested. Several newspapers were forced to close.[87] One of the several Alien Acts, the Alien Friends Act, empowered the President to deport any resident alien that he felt was "dangerous to the peace and safety of the United States."[88] It was aimed largely at French refugees and Irish immigrants who had participated in political protests against the Adams administration.[89] Although the Federalists prepared lists of aliens to be deported, President Adams refrained from signing a single deportation order. Most French residents fled the U.S. when the political climate became hostile towards France.

Such despotic legislation prompted Thomas Jefferson and Madison to remonstrate in the Kentucky and Virginia resolutions, respectively. In the latter, Madison assailed the Alien Acts:

> Could a power be well given in terms less definite,
> less particular, and less precise? To be dangerous to the
> public safety; to be suspected of secret machinations
> against the government: these can never be mistaken
> for legal rules or certain definitions. They leave every
> thing [sic] to the President. His will is the law.

> But it is not a Legislative power only that is given to the
> President. He is to stand in the place of the Judiciary
> also. His suspicion is the only evidence which is to
> convict: his order the only judgment which is to be

executed... It is rightly affirmed, therefore, that the act unites Legislative and Judicial powers to those of the Executive.[90]

Madison's first-hand experience with the Alien and Sedition Acts as ostensible national security responses to foreign danger informed his sermonizing: "If our nation is ever taken over, it will be taken over from within." He added: "If Tyranny and Oppression come to this land, it will be in the guise of fighting a foreign enemy."[91]

Yet, the Republic's checks and balances and republican political culture soon corrected the abusive laws. They were harshly criticized by uncowed Democratic-Republicans, The arrest of Benjamin Franklin's grandson, Benjamin Franklin Bache, under the Sedition Act evoked a public outcry.[92] A crescendo of domestic protests occasioned Abigail Adams' fear for her husband's safety. The President feared riots, and "High Federalists (the ultra-conservative wing of the party unaligned with Adams) feared bloody revolution of the French sort."[93] The oppressiveness of the Federalists' legislation contributed to their ultimate downfall.

By its terms, the statute expired in 1801 because the Federalists had no interest in protecting new President Jefferson from invective; and, Jeffersonians had no interest in reciprocating the tyranny of their political opponents. Eleven prosecutions were initiated under the Alien and Sedition Act prohibitions. Congress later apologized for trampling freedom of speech and voted compensation for the Acts' victims. President Jefferson, pardoned all Sedition and Alien Acts convictions, and terminated ongoing prosecutions. The judgment of history and the United States Supreme Court in *New York Times v. Sullivan* is that the Sedition Act was unconstitutional.

The fact that John Adams, a crowning figure amongst the Founding Fathers, would endorse a flagrantly unconstitutional law under the banner of national security exemplifies why the Constitution's makers entrusted war powers to Congress rather than the executive branch. They realized that presidents would crave and abuse wartime powers to secure their political popularity and thus concoct excuses for conflict. Writing to Thomas Jefferson, Madison observed that the Constitution "supposes what the History of all Governments demonstrates, that the Executive is the branch of power most interested in war and most prone to it. It has accordingly, with studied care, vested the question of war in the Legislature."[94]

In contrast to the President, Members of Congress have no incentive for warfare. Members are not Commander in Chief. They do not earn laurels for winning or fighting a war. It does not crown Members with fame, money, secrecy, appointments, or the thrill of seeking a world transformation. Nor does it grant them emergency powers to freeze assets or detain politically unpopular minorities. President Franklin D. Roosevelt earned political kudos for herding 120,000 Japanese Americans into concentration camps during World War II.

All of the latter muscular powers enjoyed by the President in wartime create an irresistible presidential incentive to inflate dangers to justify war, to deceive Congress and the American people to obtain their approval or acceptance of military conflict, and, to manipulate facts to justify belligerency. The President is characteristically tantalized by the prospect of eternal fame and remembrance by dominating the world with a Julius Caesar-like boast: Veni, Vedi, Vici. Thus, the Constitution's makers made Congress, not the President, the sole authority to initiate war.

The Constitution authorized the House of Representatives to impeach and the Senate to convict and remove a president for deceiving Congress to obtain a declaration of war. James Iredell, at the North Carolina constitutional ratification convention, maintained that the President would certainly be impeached for withholding information from Congress to elicit its support for war or other measures, which would not have been forthcoming if the true facts had been known.

The United States Supreme Court sustained the supremacy of Congress over the President in matters of war and peace in *Little .v Barreme* (1804). There, Chief Justice John Marshall held that during the United

States quasi-conflict with France, President John Adams had exceeded his powers as Commander in Chief in seizing an American ship that departed from a foreign port. Congress had only authorized interdictions of vessels that had sailed from the United States; and, Congress was the final word. In *Brown v. United States* (1814), Chief Justice Marshall further held that only Congress was empowered to order the condemnation of enemy property in the United States at the commencement of war. It was not an inherent presidential power to be exercised as Commander in Chief.

Conflicts with the Barbary States in the early 19th century did not contradict the principles of neutrality, defense against foreign aggression, or the supremacy of Congress in national security affairs expounded in the Charter Documents. Military force was employed to end piracy—a universal crime. Force was not used to extend freedom to North Africa or to gain an economic advantage over rival trading nations. The Barbary States, not the American Republic, declared war and initiated hostilities. Congress enacted nine statutes authorizing President Thomas Jefferson to use military force against the Barbary Pirates to secure open sea lanes. After obtaining authority from Congress, President Jefferson and then President Madison employed military force to protect United States citizens and to safeguard America's neutral commerce.

The Louisiana Purchase of 1803 did not flout the philosophy of the Charter Documents. The territory acquired (which constituted portions of 14 current States) was slated for self-government, statehood and representation in Congress and the White House. The Purchase did not seek domination or subjugation of new subjects.

The War of 1812 also harmonized with the nation's Charter Documents. On June 19, 1812, President Madison officially declared war on England *at the direction of an act of Congress*. In speaking to the legislative branch asking for a state of belligerency, Madison amplified:

> Whether the United States shall continue passive [not to take any action]...or, opposing force to force in

> defense of their national rights, shall commit a just cause
> into the hands of the Almighty Disposer of Events...is
> a solemn question which the Constitution wisely con-
> fides to the legislative department of the Government.
> In recommending it to their early deliberations I am
> happy in the assurance that the decision will be worthy
> of the enlightened and patriotic councils of a virtuous,
> a free, and a powerful nation.[95]

America's declaration of war answered repeated British assaults against United States' citizens, its sovereignty, and commerce. This included the impressments or kidnappings of American sailors by the British navy, British violation of American neutrality, the blockade of U.S. ports, and British refusal to revoke the orders that prevented foreign ships from trading in America. The War of 1812 was neither an offensive nor preemptive war.

The Charter Documents champion government in the sunshine and frown on secrecy. Executive privilege or state secrets are nowhere mentioned in the Constitution's text. The decision to expose the debacle of the Arthur St. Clair Expedition is yet another example of Congress' initial fidelity to the ideals presented in the Farewell Address.[96] Executive privilege was asserted only once by President George Washington to deny the House of Representatives treaty negotiating documents that President Washington had previously shared with the Senate.

By the time the Empire soared to its apex after 9/11, President George W. Bush refused to permit presidential advisers to *appear* before congressional committees to answer questions or respond to document requests. President Obama refused to permit his *social secretary* to appear to testify about arriviste White House party crashers. In domestic affairs, the Federal Reserve Board spends trillions of dollars with no congressional audit. A presumption of executive branch secrecy has replaced a presumption of transparency. Never in the history of the United States have the people and Congress known and demanded so little about so much of what the executive branch is doing.

President James Monroe, in his December 1823 State of the Union Message to Congress, praised government in the sunshine as essential to self-government and a corrective to ill-conceived government judgments from ulterior motives:

> ...The people being with us exclusively the sovereign, it is indispensable that full information be laid before them on all important subjects, to enable them to exercise that high power with complete effect. If kept in the dark, they must be incompetent to it. We are all liable to error, and those who are engaged in the management of public affairs are more subject to excitement, and to be led astray by their particular interests and passions, then the great body of our constituents, who, living at home, in pursuit of their ordinary avocations, are calm but deeply interested spectators of events, and of the conduct of those who are parties to them. To the people, every Department of the Government, and every individual in each, are responsible, and the more full their information, the better they can judge of the wisdom of the policy pursued, and the conduct of each in regard to it. From their dispassionate judgment, much aid may always be obtained, while their approbation will form the greatest incentive, and most gratifying reward, for virtuous actions, and the dread of their censure the best security against abuse of their confidence. Their interests, in all vital questions, are the same, and the bond of sentiment, as well as by interest, will be proportionately strengthened as they are better

informed of the real state of public affairs, especially in difficult conjectures.[97]

During the Golden Age of the American Republic, no state secrets privilege shielding government officials from legal accountability for wrongdoing in civil litigation was ever claimed. The privilege was born by the United States Supreme Court in *Totten v. United States* (1875). In that case, the Court held that a government contract to undertake espionage implicitly carried an obligation to keep the contract confidential. Thus, suit could not be brought to enforce an agreement to spy. *Totten* did not involve classified documents, the withholding of information from Congress, or, constitutional misconduct. Moreover, the government had little incentive to renounce contractual obligations because a reputation for reneging would have driven away talented and honest spies. In contrast, the state secrets privilege in the American Empire thwarts remedies for constitutional wrongdoing by executive officials and invites repetition.

During the famous treason and misdemeanor prosecution of Aaron Burr in 1807, championed by his arch political enemy President Thomas Jefferson, Chief Justice John Marshall denied any absolute presidential claim of privilege with regard to communications to or from the President. He insisted that the ultimate determination of whether a criminal defendant enjoyed a constitutional right to examine alleged exculpatory exchanges with the President rested with the court. The Chief Justice declared that the judicial decision should be made after an in camera scrutiny of the communications. Whether to order disclosure would turn on the relevance of the communication to the defense and the threat that disclosure would embarrass the executive branch. The final decision was up to the judge, not the President.

Congress meticulously reviewed the Second Bank of the United States and the role of President Andrew Jackson in crippling its viability without being hindered by claims of executive privilege. Fueled by its findings, the Senate, in 1834, voted a censure of President Andrew

Jackson as follows: "Resolved that the President, in the late executive proceedings in relation to the public revenue, has assumed upon himself authority and power not conferred by the constitution and laws, but in derogation of both."[98]

In accord with the Charter Documents, the American Republic practiced moderation and neutrality towards all nations irrespective of their political dispensations. It had no ambition to remake the world in its own image. The Constitution's makers believed that the sumum bonum of the human endeavor, i.e. freedom, should be participation, individually or collectively, directly or through representatives, in the enactment of laws for the governing of all evenhandedly. They would have disparaged American Idol or the Super Bowl as drivel.

The Founding Fathers recognized that the human species instinctively associates greatness with conquest and dominance of the world through military projection. But they profoundly disagreed with that puerile conception of national purpose. They believed that power for the sake of power was an unworthy goal, analogous to a lion's wish to rule the jungle. They celebrated the virtues of restraint and humility, epitomized by George Washington's refusal to even consider kingship. They were content to secure the blessings of liberty for themselves and their posterity, and they knew an educated and mature public opinion was indispensable to that end.

The Charter Documents enjoyed relatively short shelf lives. After the first political generations died or were eclipsed, the Republic began to flirt with initiating wars exhorted by Presidents seeking glory and power. The political culture began to trumpet manifest destiny as justification for the United States to control or dominate the world in order to uplift mankind. The march of the Republic towards Empire variously accelerated and decelerated after the 1846-1848 Mexican-American War, but it never ceased. The last serious protest was an 85-81 vote in 1848 by the House of Representatives to censure President Polk for "unnecessarily and unconstitutionally" beginning the conflict.

AMERICAN EMPIRE: BEFORE THE FALL

Despite their clarity and genius, the ideas celebrated in the nation's Charter Documents are resisted by the American Empire's political leaders and citizens. Any challenge to prevailing ways of thinking or vested economic or political interests triggers anxieties or alarm. The Charter Documents teach that the United States would be safer, freer, and wealthier by ending all international military entanglements and withdrawing all its troops and military advisers from more than 135 foreign countries, including Iraq, Afghanistan, Pakistan, Yemen, Germany, Japan, South Korea, and Guantanamo Bay, Cuba. But removing the nation's military footprint abroad will upset the economic interests of the military-terrorism-industrial complex and numerous military, political, and academic careers. The latter fortress of vested interests will fight fiercely to retain or to enlarge a military-counter-terrorism posture that advances their private selfish interests. Think of how Members of Congress and private military suppliers chronically advocate in favor of weapons systems unwanted even by the Pentagon because both extravagant and irrelevant to national security.

In sum, fidelity to the Charter Documents would require a complete revamping of the nation's national security strategy. All U.S. troops stationed abroad would be withdrawn. Every treaty or executive agreement obligating the United States to defend any other country from attack, including the United Nations charter would be renounced. Congress would enjoy access to every scrap of information or advice held in the executive branch. Pre-emptive wars or wars against non-state actors would cease. And strict neutrality towards all nations, an impenetrable defense cordon around the United States, and a crushing retaliatory capacity pledged to incinerate any aggressor would be embraced.

4

America's Descent into Empire:
From the Mexican-American
War to World War II

As time went on, the Republic's Charter Documents steadily lost their influence on the American people. These were progressively replaced by a squalid and juvenile culture that celebrated control or domination for the sake of domination, action for the sake of action, and status for the sake of status. In the years that post-dated the Founding era, egalitarianism and the common man replaced an aristocracy of merit and men of genius as the nation's signature. This alarming degeneration found expression in the mediocrity or worse that came to earmark the nation's political and non-political leaders. Thus, Alexis de Tocqueville, writing in *Democracy in America* in 1831, lamented: "The race of American statesman has evidently dwindled most remarkably in the course of the last fifty years."[99]

The signatories of the Declaration of Independence and the makers of the Constitution were brilliantly educated and philosophically mature: Washington, Franklin, Adams, Hamilton, Jefferson, Madison, Mason, Henry, Wilson, Randolph, etc. Their erudite learning found expression in part in *The Federalist Papers* and the *Annals of Congress*. Renowned politician

Lord Gladstone, a four time Prime Minister of the United Kingdom, effused, "[T]he American Constitution is the most wonderful work ever struck off at a given time by the brain and purpose of man."[100] John Adams pronounced the Constitution "if not the greatest exertion of human understanding...the greatest single effort of national deliberation that the world has ever seen."[101] Thomas Jefferson agreed that the Constitution was "unquestionably the wisest ever yet presented to man."[102]

The Founding Fathers understood that what distinguished man from animal was a capacity for self-government based on principles of due process, freedom of speech, and equality under the law. They provided the leadership that inspired a republican political culture vastly superior to what ordinary citizens—today's hockey Mom or Joe the plumber—would achieve if left leaderless. The Republic's culture taught that the anointment of "We the People" as sovereign, with all its errors and stumbles, was preferable to comfortable vassalage under infallible Platonic guardians; that modesty and non-belligerency were superior to domination or conquest; that thinking should precede acting; and that liberty, due process, and justice are hallmarks of national greatness. Indeed, James Madison sermonized in *Federalist 51*: "Justice is the end of government. It is the end of civil society. It ever has been and ever will be pursued until it be obtained, or until liberty be lost in the pursuit."[103] And John Stuart Mill lectured in the spirit of the Constitution: "It is better to be a human being dissatisfied than a pig satisfied; better to be Socrates dissatisfied than a fool satisfied. And if the fool, or the pig, are a different opinion, it is because they only know their own side of the question."[104]

Moreover, as the nation would not be a colony, the Founding Fathers advised, so it should not be a colonizer. They concurred with Edward Gibbon's observation in *The History of the Decline and Fall of the Roman Empire* that, "There is nothing more adverse to nature and reason than to hold in obedience remote *countries and foreign nations, in opposition to their inclination and interest.*"[105] The attempt to enforce obedience would squander military and economic resources and provoke deep resentments among the indigenous peoples who would become enemies of the occupying power.

AMERICA'S DESCENT INTO EMPIRE

The Founding Fathers' successors became progressively less educated, and suspicious or disdainful of extraordinary talent and statesmanship. Their actions and ambitions plunged from adult to adolescent. The ignorant find gratification in power over others and are unable to perceive a higher purpose in life beyond the primal urges of fame, money, and sex. The Republic's high-minded leadership that inspired citizens to rise above their appetites and hedonistic pleasures through example and exhortation yielded to non-leader leaders who excited and propitiated the base instincts of commoners.

The change in the political culture was born of the commendable leveling of society through diffusion of political power, non-discrimination, and equal justice under law. Extension of the franchise to non-property owners was one manifestation. Unfortunately, the result was a cultural egalitarian juggernaut in which mediocrity and the lowest common denominator brought forth the richest political, economic, and cultural rewards.

President Andrew Jackson was elected in 1832 to succeed the learned and long-headed John Quincy Adams, the last of the founding generation to occupy the White House. Jackson was a crude and ill-educated man with a sparkling record of military triumphs marred by sacrileges to the Great Writ of habeas corpus, due process, and civilian supremacy. He preached that ignorant farmers could discharge government responsibilities as adeptly as the wisest Socrates or Solon. His model of political leadership and citizenry was a rude frontiersman born in a log cabin who fought Indians and drank hard cider. Scorned was the wise, humble, and prudent statesman capable of leading, informing, and persuading rather than echoing popular opinion. The last of this class were Daniel Webster, Henry Clay, John C. Calhoun, and Thomas Hart Benton.

A stream of mediocrities followed Mr. Jackson into the White House: Martin Van Buren, William Henry Harrison, John Tyler, Zachery Taylor, Franklin Pierce, and James Buchanan. Harrison's campaign slogan—Tippecanoe and Tyler too—epitomized the political culture's regression into infantilism. With the exception of President Abraham Lincoln, the

White House for the remainder of the nineteenth century was filled with men who could have contributed little or nothing to the Constitutional Convention of 1787: Andrew Johnson; U.S. Grant, Rutherford B. Hayes, James A. Garfield, Chester A. Arthur, Grover Cleveland, Benjamin Harrison, and William McKinley. As public ignorance of the charter documents grew, The American Republic began to yield to an American Empire fueled by a growing military profile.

The Monroe Doctrine of 1823 represented the Republic's initial crack. It warned European powers against any new colonization of the Americas and subtly threatened war if its admonition went unheeded. The Farewell Address, in contrast, championed strict neutrality and formidable defenses rather than any extension of the nation's defense perimeter beyond its borders. President Washington would never have contemplated war if France sought to colonize Argentina or Venezuela after their respective emancipations from Spain. The Monroe Doctrine was dubious on its face in any event. When it was announced, Canada was a colony of Great Britain, and Cuba was a colony of Spain. Yet neither act of colonization threatened United States sovereignty or prosperity.

The Charter Documents were profaned by the emergence of "Manifest Destiny," a euphemism for dominating other nations by military force or conquest. The creed originated in the writings of John L. O'Sullivan, an influential American journalist and founding editor of *The United States Magazine and Democratic Review.*" It espoused the territorial expansion of the United States in the 1840s.[106] In 1845, O'Sullivan wrote "Annexation," an article focusing on the possible acquisition of Texas and California, stating that foreign nations are intruding in the affairs of these territories...

> for the avowed object of thwarting our policy and hampering our power, limiting our greatness and checking the fulfillment of our manifest destiny to overspread the continent allotted by Providence for the free development of our yearly multiplying millions...The

Anglo-Saxon foot is already on [California's] borders. Already the advance guard of the irresistible army of Anglo-Saxon emigration has begun to pour down upon it...The day is not distant when the Empires of the Atlantic and the Pacific would again flow together into one...[107]

The jingoistic, expansionist doctrine of Manifest Destiny was further captured in O'Sullivan's December 1, 1845 editorial for the *New York Morning News*. It declared that the United States had a divine right to take Oregon County from Canada because America had proven superior in civilizing the frontier through development and enlightenment. The editorial further proclaimed the duty of the United States to shield every nation in the world from domination by European powers. O'Sullivan perceived America as destined and duty-bound to uplift all mankind. It should never be satisfied with its mission, as enshrined in the Constitution, of merely securing the blessings of liberty to ourselves and our posterity. Indeed, he maintained that God had anointed the United States to alleviate misery around the globe—or at least in the western hemisphere. The language he employed was a direct descendant of the Pope's exhortations to the Crusaders to liberate Jerusalem. It persists as the spirit of the American Empire. It finds expression in President Obama's insistence that the United States is obligated to intervene anywhere in the world to prevent genocide or comparable atrocities, and that the United States must employ the instruments of war to secure peace in every nook and cranny of the planet. And to Sarah Palin, Obama's vision is too modest and unassertive.

O'Sullivan's editorial elaborated:

A wise and merciful Providence has guided our course, nourished our growth, increased our vigor, and each day poured new blessings upon our heads. But with all, has no 'mission' been given for us to fulfill? Has the privilege been also added to shut our eyes and stop our ears and steel our hearts to human woes and human wrongs, and man's abasement? Are we to know or seek naught but our own enjoyment? Shall we virtually say to the monarchies of Europe leave us but the Lakes for our Northern border, and the Rocky Mountains on the West, and take all else to gorge your insatiable appetite for increased dominion, rule it with the rod of rigor, and choke down the first aspiration for freedom in all its vast extent? Or shall we, with the eye of faith fixed on the glowing future, and love for our kind warm in our hearts, ask Great Britain and every other power, what need have you, three thousand miles away, of another slice of man's inheritance in the New World? Shall we not say to them, 'this territory must be secured for civilized man and free institutions; we will keep it open for settlement by all who seek it, as well as for your subjects, panting for a breath of untaxed air, as for our own citizens. The privileges and advantages granted unto us impose an equitable obligation to endeavor to extend their bountiful blessings to the whole human race.[108]

With the memories of the Founding Fathers waning, few leaders or intellects opposed Manifest Destiny in favor of the Charter Documents. One exception, William E. Channing was a disciple of the Founding generation. In an 1837 letter to Henry Clay, he wrote:

Did this country know itself, or were it disposed to profit by self-knowledge, it would feel the necessity of laying an immediate curb on its passion for extended

> territory....We are a restless people, prone to encroach-
> ment, impatient of the ordinary laws of progress...We
> boast of our rapid growth, forgetting that, throughout
> nature, noble growths are slow.... It is full time that
> we should lay on ourselves serious, resolute restraint.
> Possessed of a domain, vast enough for the growth of
> ages, it is time for us to stop in the career of acquisition
> and conquest. Already endangered by our greatness, we
> cannot advance without imminent peril to our institu-
> tions, union, prosperity, virtue, and peace....[109]

Despite Channing's warning, "Manifest Destiny"—a doctrine trea-
sonous to the Charter Documents—became the organizing principle
of America's national security and foreign policy. It made the American
Empire inescapable: an ambition to save all mankind from tyranny; a belief
that Divine Providence desired nothing less; a conviction that the United
States was superior morally, politically, economically, and culturally to
any other country; and a craving to dominate the world. The United States
would no longer rest content to influence the world by the force of example. Such restraint lacked the animalistic virility that Americans now
increasingly viewed as the earmark of a healthy civilization.

Manifest Destiny's imperialistic drum echoed the themes of the British
Empire at its apex. Winston Churchill, in his first political speech delivered
after Queen Victoria's Jubilee in 1897, assailed voices who prophesied the
Empire's decline like Rome. Churchill urged the British to:

> ...not believe these croakers but give the lie to their
> dismal croaking by showing by our actions that the
> vigor and vitality of our race is unimpaired and that
> our determination is to uphold the Empire that we have
> inherited from our fathers as Englishmen (cheers), that

our flag shall fly high upon the sea, our voice be heard
in the councils of Europe, our Sovereign supported by
the love of her subjects, then shall we continue to pursue that course marked out for us by an all-wise hand
and carry out our mission of bearing peace, civilization and good government to the uttermost ends of the
earth (Loud cheers).[110]

Britain then thought it was bearing the White Man's burden to civi-
lize Asia and the world. It chronically fought wars for nothing more than
the psychic gratification of domination. A century would elapse before it
was America's turn to succumb to this debased human ambition.

A year after O'Sullivan coined the term "Manifest Destiny," the
United States Congress, with the mendacious prodding of President
James K. Polk, declared war on Mexico to launch the Mexican-American
War of 1846-1848. The conflict marked the first occasion when American
leaders wielded military power for the sake of domination. It began the
nation down a ruinous and unstoppable path towards Empire. For the first
time, the President would deceive Congress and the American people to
justify belligerency. The constitutional disease became chronic.

Consumed with controlling more territory and a greater population,
President Polk duped the voters and Members of Congress in his May 11,
1846 address to Congress asking for authority to commence war against
Mexico. He falsely accused Mexican soldiers of killing American servicemen on American soil and of initiating war:

Meantime Texas, by the final action of our Congress,
had become an integral part of our Union. The
Congress of Texas, by its act of December 19, 1836,
had declared the Rio del Norte to be the boundary of
that Republic...The country between that river and the

Del Norte had been represented in the Congress and in the convention of Texas, and thus taken part in the act of annexation itself, and is now included within one of our Congressional districts...The movement of the troops to the Del Norte was made by the commanding general under positive instructions to abstain from all aggressive acts toward Mexico or Mexican citizens and to regard the relations between that Republic and the United States as peaceful unless she should declare war or commit acts of hostility indicative of a state of war...But now, after reiterated menaces, Mexico has passed the boundary of the United States, has invaded our territory and shed American blood upon the American soil. She has proclaimed that hostilities have commenced, and that the two nations are now at war. As war exists, and, notwithstanding all our efforts to avoid it, exists by the act of Mexico herself, we are called upon by every consideration of duty and patriotism to vindicate with decision the honor, the rights, and the interests of our country.[111]

In truth, the Mexican military killed American soldiers in Mexican territory after the United States waged a campaign of belligerency against Mexico. The Mexican government had not proclaimed war first.

Congressman Abraham Lincoln openly disputed Polk's falsehoods. He introduced his famous "Spot Resolutions" to the House of Representatives on December 22, 1847, challenging the President to identify the spot of undisputed American soil where Mexican forces allegedly killed United States soldiers. His detractors, in a manner reminiscent of contemporary politicians, criticized his challenge as endangering American soldiers during wartime. His resolution predictably received short shrift in the House of Representatives. A month after it sputtered, Lincoln argued:

If the President can show that the soil was ours where the first blood of the war was shed then I am with him for his justification. But if he cannot or will not do this then I shall be fully convinced of what I more than suspect already – that he is deeply conscious of being in the wrong; that he feels the blood of this war, like the blood of Abel, is crying to Heaven against him; that originally having some strong motive – what, I will not stop now to give my opinion concerning – to involve the two countries in a war, and trusting to escape scrutiny by fixing the public gaze upon the exceeding brightness of military glory – that attractive rainbow that rises in showers of blood – that serpent's eye that charms to destroy – he plunged into it, and has swept on and on till, disappointed in his calculation of the ease with which Mexico might be subdued, he now finds himself he knows not where.[112]

While Congress scoffed at Lincoln's resolution, one erstwhile and one future president shared his disparagement of the Mexican-American War. Then Congressman Quincy Adams and former president led the tiny Whig opposition and voted against what he referred to as "a most unrighteous war."[113] Ulysses S. Grant, later General of the Army of the Potomac and President of the United States, served as Second Lieutenant in the Mexican-American conflict. He wrote in his War Memoirs: "[The War was] one of the most unjust ever waged by a stronger against a weaker nation. It was an instance of a republic following the bad example of European monarchies, in not considering justice in their desire to acquire additional territory."[114]

Polk followed his May 1846 address to Congress with another speech on December 8, 1846, where he asserted that war with Mexico was necessary to prevent a European power from installing a monarchy in Mexico and introducing European-like balance of power politics into the American continent. He maintained:

Besides, there was good reason to believe from [Mexican President Paredes'] conduct that it was his intention to convert the Republic of Mexico into a monarchy and to call a foreign European prince to the throne. Preparatory to that end, he had during his short rule destroyed the liberty of the press, tolerating that portion of it only which openly advocated establishment of a monarchy.[115]

Such an inflated fear of European monarchy in Mexico was summoned to justify the President's demand for hostilities against Mexico. Joel Roberts Poinsett, the first United States Minister to Mexico and former U.S. Secretary of War under President Martin Van Buren, commented on the absurdity of Polk's ostensible worry:

The President is apprehensive of foreign interference, first in California, and next in the establishment of a monarchy in Mexico. There is not the slightest risk of the former, and, if the Mexican people are left to themselves, no chance of the latter...[T]he President is wrong; our armed intervention might bring on us a powerful foreign foe but could not prevent the evil; whereas if we hold back...a monarchy could not exist in Mexico three years....The people are Republican.[116]

Not a crumb of evidence indicated that Mexico was endangering the sovereignty of the United States when Polk addressed Congress. The war had nothing to do with securing the blessings of liberty for living Americans or for their posterity—the exclusive task of the Government of the United States ordained by the nation's Charter Documents.

AMERICAN EMPIRE: BEFORE THE FALL

The Mexican-American War concluded with the Treaty of Guadalupe-Hidalgo. It yielded substantial territorial gains for the United States, including California, New Mexico, Arizona, and Nevada, in exchange for a payment of $15 million and the assumption of American citizen damage claims against Mexico exceeding $3 million.

While dormant during the American Civil War of 1861-1865, the principles of Manifest Destiny and the psychology of Empire revived afterwards as a staple of the United States political culture. Five years after the Civil War ended, President Ulysses S. Grant urged the United States Congress to annex the country of Santo Domingo (now the Dominican Republic) for a naval base and place of residency for southern blacks.[117] Although the Senate refused to ratify the treaty in 1870, the mentality of Empire was in full gear as the United States sought military or territorial expansion.

The Spanish-American War of 1898 was emblematic. In the mid-1890s, the United States public clamored for the government to end the violence and alleged atrocities committed by Spanish forces against Cuban nationals in the tumultuous Spanish-controlled Cuba. American manufactured apprehensions reached a fever pitch following the destruction of the USS *Maine* on February 15, 1898 in Cuba's Havana harbor. More than 260 American sailors were killed. While originally opposed to armed intervention on the island, after the sinking of the USS *Maine,* President McKinley bowed to the prevailing political winds.

Nearly two months after the destruction of the vessel, he sought congressional authority to initiate war against Spain over Cuba. During his speech to Congress on April 11th, 1898, he misrepresented the evidence tending to exonerate the Government of Spain from any complicity in the USS Maine explosion, and articulated reasons for war that had been repudiated in the nation's Charter Documents:

> The naval court of inquiry, which, it is needless to say; commands the unqualified confidence of the

Government, was unanimous in its conclusion that the destruction of the Maine was caused by an exterior explosion – that of a submarine mine. It did not assume to place the responsibility. That remains to be fixed. In any event, the destruction of the Maine, by whatever exterior cause, is a patent and impressive proof of a state of things in Cuba that is intolerable. That condition is thus shown to be such that the Spanish Government cannot assure safety and security to a vessel of the American Navy in the harbor of Havana on a mission of peace, and rightfully there.[118]

There were conflicting accounts and explanations surrounding the sinking of the naval ship. The Spanish insisted it was occasioned by an internal explosion, based on its own investigation of the debris and collection of eyewitness accounts. An investigation by four-star admiral Hyman G. Rickover of the US Navy in 1976 supported the Spanish claim. Even if President McKinley was correct and the destruction of the *Maine* was the result of an external explosion, there was no evidence to suggest that Spain or Spanish loyalists placed the mine. Cuban rebels were also motivated to destroy the *Maine*, as its destruction would undoubtedly draw the United States deeper into the conflict. Further, the Founding Fathers sanctioned war only in response to an attack against the sovereignty of the United States, not because of domestic convulsions in the colony of a foreign government that might endanger American lives or property there. The latter can be protected by military force without initiating war.

President McKinley signed a joint war resolution on April 20th, 1898, followed by an ultimatum to Spain that unless the colonial power relinquished its authority over Cuba by noon on April 23, the United States would use force to implement the terms of the congressional resolution. McKinley signed the U.S. Congressional declaration of war on April 25th, 1898.

Regarding the situation in Cuba, the President stated in his earlier address to Congress on April 11th, 1898: "Of the untried measures there remains only one:...I speak not of forcible annexation, for that cannot be thought of. That, by our code of morality, would be criminal aggression."[119] He also stated on February 16th, 1899, "no imperial designs lurk in the American mind. They are alien to American sentiment, thought, and purpose."[120] President McKinley's actions both belied his statements and exemplified America's imperial psychology at play. While declining to annex Cuba outright following Spain's defeat in early 1899, the United Stated did bring within its sovereignty the Philippines, Guam, and Puerto Rico. Further, the United States circumscribed Cuba's foreign policy and established a perpetual lease and dominion over Guantanamo Bay.[121] It was altogether fitting that Guantanamo Bay Naval Base, acquired initially due to an Empire psychology, would later serve as the American Empire's post-9/11 prison for detainees indefinitely held as enemy combatants without accusation or trial in the perpetual and global war against international terrorism.

President McKinley's touting of the civilizing, psychic, and economic benefit of annexing the Philippines further demonstrated his American Empire mindset. Speaking to a crowd in Iowa in the fall of 1898, he elaborated, "Territory sometimes comes to us when we go to war for a holy cause, and whenever it does the banner of liberty will float over it and bring, I trust, blessings and benefits to all the people."[122] Before another crowd he amplified, "We have pretty much everything in this country to make it happy. We have good money, we have ample revenues, we have unquestioned national credit; but we want new markets, and as trade follows the flag, it looks very much as if we were going to have new markets." Finally, he exclaimed to a crowd in Illinois, "When you cannot sell your broom-corn in our own country, you are glad to send the surplus to some other country, and get their good money for your good broom-corn."[123]

According to Susan Brewer, author of "Why America Fights," McKinley stated to a circle of intimates at the Executive Mansion:

AMERICA'S DESCENT INTO EMPIRE

> One of the best things we ever did was to insist upon taking the Philippines and not a coaling station or an island, for if we had done the latter we would have been the laughing stock of the world…And so it has come to pass that in a few short months we have become a world power.[124]

As the 1800s concluded, a growing imperial mentality dominated the American psyche, with its appetite for power and expansion paralleling its ballooning economic and military strength. The early 20th century witnessed the steady expansion of presidential power in tandem with chronic American interventions in Central and South America. In 1903, then Attorney General Philander Knox would retort to President Theodore Roosevelt's request for a legal defense of the United States annexation of the Panama Canal and severance of Panama from Columbia by the use of military force decreed by the President alone: "Mr. President, do not let so great an achievement suffer from any taint of legality."[125]

U.S. Marines occupied Nicaragua from 1912-1925, and 1926-1933, respectively, to protect United States financial interests, the option to pursue a Nicaraguan canal route, and to suppress opposition to a friendly Nicaraguan government. The twin U.S. Marine occupations were wholly superfluous to the nation's safety, freedom, or wealth. The financial risk of political instability in a foreign country can be addressed through insurance or other private market mechanisms. The United States military and the American taxpayer should play no part in protecting imprudent foreign investments. President William Howard Taft defended the military intervention in Nicaragua as follows:

> During this last revolution in Nicaragua, the government of that republic having admitted its inability to protect American life and property against acts of sheer lawlessness on the part of the malcontents, and

having requested this government to assume that office, it became necessary to land over 2,000 Marines
and Bluejackets in Nicaragua. Owing to their presence
the constituted government of Nicaragua was free to
devote its attention wholly to its internal troubles, and
was thus enabled to stamp out the rebellion in a short
space of time.[126]

The United States intervened in the affairs of the Dominican Republic
between 1912 and 1924. Earlier, in 1905, the United States assumed the
administration of Dominican customs to pay off foreign creditors. In 1912,
the United States dispatched 750 Marines there following the assassination of the Dominican President Ramon Caceres; denied the Dominican
Republic funds from the customs receivership; and installed Adolfo Nouel
as the new president.[127] The United States forced the succeeding president, Jose Bordas, to resign in 1914. The U.S. military intervened to support President Juan Isidro Jimenez on May 7, 1916. Finally, the United
States deposed the Dominican government on November 29th, 1916 in
favor of direct U.S. military rule.[128] Its occupation and administration of
the Dominican Republic over exaggerated fears of a German takeover to
launch war against the United States endured from 1916 to 1924.

The United States entry into World War I in 1917 featured the utopian
mission of making the world safe for democracy, which the war assuredly
did not. Instead, the war proved the antechamber for Hitler, Mussolini,
Lenin, and Stalin. Deceit of the American people by inflating danger or
misrepresenting the enemy played its customary starring role. The sinking of the civilian ocean liner RMS *Lusitania* by a German U-boat on May
7, 1915, while less influential than the Zimmerman Telegram, fueled
American public opinion towards war. Germany correctly insisted that the
Lusitania was not an innocent vessel. According to the German leadership,
it was transporting military equipment and Canadian troops destined for
the front lines against Germany. President Wilson mendaciously retorted:

Of the facts alleged in Your Excellency's note, if true, the Government of the United States would have been bound to take official cognizance in performing its recognized duty as a neutral power and in enforcing its national laws. It was its duty to see to it that the Lusitania was not armed for offensive action, that she was not serving as a transport, that she did not carry a cargo prohibited by the statutes of the United States, and that, if in fact she was a naval vessel of Great Britain, she should not receive clearance as a merchantman, and it performed that duty and enforced its statutes with scrupulous vigilance through its regularly constituted officials. It is able, therefore, to assure the Imperial German Government that it has been misinformed... The principal fact is that a great steamer, primarily and chiefly an conveyance for passengers, and carrying more than a thousand souls who had no part or lot in the conduct of the war, was torpedoed and sunk without so much as a challenge or a warning, and that men, women, and children were sent to their death in circumstances unparalleled in modern warfare.[129]

Wilson's statement was false. The *Lusitania*, while not transporting Canadian troops, carried munitions and weaponry for use against German troops. Some estimates claim that the passenger ship had 1,250 cases of 3.3-inch shrapnel shells with a total weight of 52 tons, with each box containing four shells making a total quantity of 5,000 shells.[130] The ship was also suspected of transporting 3,240 brass percussion fuses, which are necessary for 4.7-inch high explosive shells and 4,200,000 Remington rifle cartridges.[131] Wilson's fabrications over the *Lusitania* are exemplary of the readiness of the President to believe allegations that would justify war, or to mislead the American public to that end.

AMERICAN EMPIRE: BEFORE THE FALL

After World War I, the United States Empire psychology temporarily receded because of disillusionment over the war's aims and outcome. President Wilson's Fourteen Points were honored more in the breach than in the observance at the Paris Peace Conference both by himself and other leading political figures. The Senate refused to ratify the Treaty of Versailles because it threatened to engulf the United States in wars without authorization from Congress; and, a series of Neutrality Acts were passed in the 1930s to keep the nation neutral in foreign wars, which were said to be the contrivances of international bankers and munitions makers. The United States also ratified the Kellogg-Briand Treaty of 1928 featuring its blueprint for attempting to resolve every international dispute on the planet without resort to war. The Contracting Parties "condemn[ed] recourse to war for the solution of international controversies, and renounce[d] it as an instrument of national policy in their relations with one another."[132]

The inter-war years were an intermezzo in America's full transformation into Empire. But even that period witnessed the United States projection of military power into Latin America for the sake of control.

Like Polk, McKinley, and Wilson, President Franklin D. Roosevelt was eager for the United States to enter into war before any threat to U.S. sovereignty had emerged, whether from the Third Reich, Japan, or otherwise. His willingness to deceive the American public to justify war was highlighted in the so-called "Greer Incident." In a September 4, 1941 fireside chat, FDR fraudulently misrepresented an encounter between the USS *Greer* and a Germany U-boat:

> The Navy Department of the United States has reported to me that on the morning of September fourth the United States destroyer Greer, proceeding in full daylight toward Iceland, had reached a point southeast of Greenland. She was carrying American mail to Iceland. She was flying the American flag. Her identity as an American ship was unmistakable.

She was then and there attacked by a submarine. Germany admits that it was a German submarine. The submarine deliberately fired a torpedo at the Greer, followed later by another torpedo attack. In spite of what Hitler's propaganda bureau has invented, and in spite of what any American obstructionist organization may prefer to believe, I tell you the blunt fact that the German submarine fired upon this American destroyer without warning and with deliberate design to sink her. This was piracy – piracy legally and morally...[I]t would be inexcusable folly to minimize such incidents in the face of evidence which makes it clear that the incident is not isolated, but is part of a general plan...Hitler's advance guards – not only his avowed agents but also his dupes among us – have sought to make ready for him footholds and bridgeheads in the New World, to be used as soon as he has gained control of the oceans.[133]

Admiral Harold Stark, Chief of Naval Operation, exposed FDR's wild prevarication before the Senate Naval Affairs Committee:

At 8:40 AM on the morning of September 4, 1941 the USS Greer was notified by a British airplane that a submerged German U-boat was in the path of the destroyer about ten miles ahead. The Greer raced to the location using its sonar detection equipment and while tracking the U-boat began relaying the information to British airplanes. At 10:32 AM a British airplane began dropping depth charges on the location of the U-boat, but was unsuccessful and withdrew. The Greer continued tracking the submarine until at 12:40 PM

the U-boat ceased fleeing, turned on the Greer and
fired a torpedo that missed. The Greer counterattacked
with depth charges and the U-boat responded with
torpedoes. The entire episode lasted four hours during
which time the Greer pursued the fleeing submarine
for over three hours. The U-boat attempted to avoid
the American vessel, but was relentlessly pursued by
the American craft.[134]

Based on the Admiral's account, the German U-boat fired on the USS
Greer in self-defense. President Roosevelt blatantly lied in painting the
incident as part of a German campaign to attack and destroy American
vessels.

A sister presidential lie sallied forth when a German U-boat scored
a direct hit against the USS *Kearney* in the North Atlantic, severely dam-
aging the ship and killing many. Roosevelt maintained that the German
vessel fired without provocation. He insisted on October 27th, "We have
wished to avoid shooting. But the shooting has started. And history has
recorded who fired the first shot…America has been attacked."[135] The
truth was different. A German U-boat fired at the USS *Kearney* after the
American warship had rescued merchant ships under attack by a German
U-boat "wolf pack" and repeatedly dropped depth charges on the Nazi
submarines. The German response was self-defense, not unprovoked
aggression.[136]

Once again, America's cultural and political leaders succumbed to the
imperial psychosis of their predecessors. Life Magazine publisher Henry
Luce immortalized the persistent prevalence of the American passion for
dominance in his 1941 editorial effusing over The American Century: "We
must accept whole-heartedly our duty and our opportunity as the most
powerful and vital nation in the world and in consequence to exert upon
the world the full impact of our influence, for such purposes as we see
fit and by such means as we see fit."[137] His writing was a more modern

expression of Manifest Destiny, complete with the familiar trappings of religious overtones[138] and thoughtless imperatives.

The victories of World War II pushed the American Empire to new heights. The nation emerged after Japan's surrender in Tokyo Bay with the most powerful military and economy in the world and a plausible capability of dominating the entire planet with a global military footprint. It gloried in power for the sake of power and in a professed moral superiority over all other peoples that it hoped to cram down their throats if they refused to imbibe the American way.

5

Twin Myths of the American Empire

America's zeal for empire reached its apex with the end of World War II and the onset of the Cold War with the Soviet Union. By 1945, the United States was the preeminent power on earth. Until 1949, it was the sole member of the nuclear club. The Soviet Union immediately strove to surpass the economic and military capabilities of the United States, spurred by its own imperial ambitions. The subsequent struggle between the two for global domination instilled America with a nearly irreversible attitude of Empire. But its actions were tempered by a rival superpower capable of destroying the United States and the world in a nuclear Holocaust. From the late 1940s to the end of the Cold War, United States presidents interceded all over the world to affect political, military, or economic outcomes in a mindless effort to contain or to defeat the USSR in hopes of eradicating its threat to private enterprise or democratic rule. No country was too small or inconsequential for the United States to believe its alignment with the Soviet Union would be pivotal to America's safety, freedom, or prosperity. For the first time in America's history, it began to devise a foreign policy for every nation on earth, be it Chad, Mali, Mauretania, Nepal or Fiji. This attitude prevailed when no nation in the world would have dared an offensive war against the United States.

AMERICAN EMPIRE: BEFORE THE FALL

At the height of its power, the Soviet Union flinched in the Cuban Missile Crisis

During America's metamorphosis into an Empire in the mid to late 20th century, the mutated US political culture summoned two false orthodoxies into being to defend the imperative of a global United States military footprint. Each represented perfidy to the Founding Fathers and their Charter Documents.

The first orthodoxy was that the United States must spread democracy and human rights throughout the world, and maintain international stability. This conviction rested on twin pillars: that America is morally obligated to guarantee international freedom and peace and that the national security of the United States depends on the vitality of democracy in foreign lands and the preservation of global order. The second orthodoxy was that a global military presence, with its ability to ensure international stability and access to resources, was indispensable to economic growth. Both orthodoxies are patent nonsense, yet both continue to dominate American thinking.

The first myth regarding the advancement of democracy and international stability originated in theories like Manifest Destiny. It took root within the American psyche following the United States electrifying experience liberating Europe and Asia from German and Japanese oppression in World War II. The United States shut its naïve eyes to the fact that its World War II allies—the Soviet Union, Great Britain, and France-were themselves oppressive Empires intent on maintaining the status quo. British Prime Minister Winston Churchill, for instance, pledged to Parliament on November 10, 1942: ``Let me, however, make this clear, in case that there should be any mistake about it in any quarter. We mean to hold our own. I have not become the King's First Minister in order to preside over the liquidation of the British Empire."[139] The Soviet Union held 15 republics in subjugation, and had snatched part of Poland and Romania and all of the Baltic States at the outset of the war pursuant to the odious Ribbentrop-Molotov Pact. France's post-war effort to retain its empire in Indochina paved the way for the United States' Vietnam War disaster.

TWIN MYTHS OF THE AMERICAN EMPIRE

Harry Truman, who became President after Franklin Roosevelt's death in 1945, echoed the orthodoxy of universal democracy and international stability as cornerstones of national security. His foreign policy principles accelerated America's departure from its Republican values and set ruinous precedents for his successors.

On March 12, 1947, a year and a half after the Allied victory over Germany and Japan, President Truman articulated the famous *Truman Doctrine* during a speech before the United States Congress. His address sought to win Congressional approval of $400 million in economic and military aid to Turkey and Greece, two countries that the executive branch viewed as being endangered by communist takeovers.

Truman simplistically conceived of the world as divided into two ways of life: one based on freedom and democratic values, and the other based on tyranny, oppression, and coercion. He elaborated that one of the primary objectives of the United States' foreign policy "…is the creation of conditions in which we and other nations will be able to work out a way of life free from coercion."[140] Truman's doctrine suggested that America must defend citizens all over the world from the coercive advances of authoritarian regimes to allow them a chance to embrace freedom and democracy. This objective, he declared, "was a fundamental issue in the war in Germany and Japan." Truman championed the United Nations as a multilateral organization essential to spreading freedom and defeating authoritarianism.[141] The President further amplified:

> I believe that it must be the policy of the United States to support free peoples who are resisting attempted subjugation by armed minorities or by outside pressures.

> I believe that we must assist free peoples to work out their own destinies in their own way.

I believe that our help should be primarily through economic and financial aid which is essential to economic stability and orderly political processes.

The world is not static, and the status quo is not sacred. But we cannot allow changes in the status quo in violation of the Charter of the United Nations by such methods as coercion, or by such subterfuges as political infiltration. In helping free and independent nations to maintain their freedom, the United States will be giving effect to the principles of the Charter of the United Nations.[142]

Presaging the false tenets of the *Domino Theory* used to justify the Vietnam War, Truman triggered alarm by claiming that communist coups in Greece or Turkey would allow totalitarianism and despair to sweep through Europe, placing the world in jeopardy: "The free people of the world look to us for support in maintaining their freedoms. If we falter in our leadership, we may endanger the peace of the world – and we shall surely endanger the welfare of this Nation."[143]

Truman's foreign policy principles betrayed the United States Charter Documents. Nothing in the text, subtext, purpose, or spirit of the Constitution authorizes the government to coerce or employ its citizens to assist in securing liberty or self-government to foreigners in a foreign country by military force or otherwise. Such a frolic could be justified only if the predictable result of the intervention would advance the constitutionally legitimate objective of securing the blessings of liberty for Americans in America. The counter-constitutional Truman Doctrine summons the philosophy of the United Nations Charter, not the nation's charter documents, for justification.

Morality—even the prevention of genocide—is a constitutionally illicit reason for initiating warfare. John Quincy Adams' July 4, 1821 address[144] and George Washington's Farewell Address explicitly reject the idea of traipsing abroad to conduct "just" or "humanitarian" wars. Additionally, the United States is not saddled with any moral obligation to alleviate oppression or genocide that the United States had no hand in creating, for instance, Zimbabweans persecuted by President Robert Mugabe, Chechens threatened by the separatist conflict with Russia, Tibetans subjugated by the Chinese Communist government, or Rwandan Tutus slaughtered by Hutus or their surrogates. Who in the United States ever felt guilty for the terrible suffering of Soviet citizens under Stalin and his successors, the horrors of Chairman Mao Zedong's Great Leap Forward and Chinese Cultural Revolution, or even the Holocaust perpetrated by Nazi Germany?

The law reflects the moral deposit of the times, and there is no obligation under international or United States law requiring nations or persons to seek to relieve oppression or war wherever it is spotted. Thus, the United States and the international community violated no law by acting as a spectator to the Rwandan genocide of 1994, the genocide from January to June 2009 of Tamil civilians in Sri Lanka by the all-Sinhalese Sri Lankan armed forces, or the continued unrest, conflict, and despotism in Myanmar. The Parable of the Good Samaritan in the Gospel of Luke has no application to nation-states. The only morality known to the United States government is honoring the Constitution—an imperative that is not discretionary. That does not suggest, however, that individuals representing only themselves might not be acclaimed for volunteering to fight for freedom abroad on behalf of oppressed peoples. The constitutional transgression arises when the United States government coerces or otherwise employs its citizens to fight in wars that are irrelevant to American sovereignty.

Contrary to the first orthodoxy, democracy abroad does not necessarily translate into enhanced American security. When the United States secured its independence from Great Britain, not a single American statesman insinuated that the nation would be made safer by seeking to transform the Ottoman Empire, the Chinese Empire, or the Russian or

French despotisms into democracies. The United States was a passive on-looker to the wars of independence in Central and South America against Spanish and Portuguese colonialist oppression. The Founding Fathers knew that democracies could easily become as belligerent as the worst of tyrannies. After independence, the United States was most endangered by Great Britain, which was then the most democratic country in the world. Indeed, Great Britain provoked the War of 1812 by impressing United States seaman and attacking neutral American ships during the Napoleonic wars. The British also burnt Washington, D.C. America was assisted during the Revolutionary War by monarchist France, which was later overthrown in the French Revolution in favor of a regime less friend-ly to the United States. The XYZ affair precipitated a naval quasi-war with France.

The first non-democratic country to initiate war against the United States was arguably Germany with its unrestricted submarine warfare in 1917. Non-democratic Japan clearly committed aggression against the United States by its attack on Pearl Harbor on December 7, 1941—more than 160 years after the nation's birth. Nazi Germany followed with a declaration of war, yet the German citizenry elected Adolph Hitler's National Socialists to power. During the entire 224 year history of the United States, Great Britain, Japan, and Germany have been the only na-tions that have initiated war against America.

In contrast, the United States, a bastion of democracy, initiated war with Mexico in the Mexican-American War. It commenced hostilities with Spain in the Spanish-American War. The United States also undertook war pursuant to a United Nations Security Council resolution against North Korea in 1950. It initiated military operations against North Vietnam in 1964, against Panama in 1989, against Iraq in 1991 and 2003, against Afghanistan in 2001, and against the entire world in pursuit of interna-tional terrorists after 9/11. The record of multiple foreign interventions by the United States undermines the idea that democratic countries will be less bellicose and less inclined to war and invasions than non-demo-cratic dispensations.

TWIN MYTHS OF THE AMERICAN EMPIRE

Great Britain's history fortifies this conclusion. After government reform crippled the power of the monarchy by the time of Queen Victoria, British wars of expansion and colonialism grew under an elected Parliament and Prime Minister. Great Britain initiated the First Afghan War (1838-42) based on a concocted need to prevent Russia from invading India. Lord Melbourne insisted that, "Afghanistan must be ours or Russia's."[145] The British fought a Second Afghan War (1878-1880) largely to retain national prestige. They fought China twice over opium (1839-1842; 1856-1860). Great Britain warred against Burma three times: 1824-1826, 1852, and 1885. The Boer War was fought from 1899-1902. Great Britain's wars against the Great Mahdi and his followers in Sudan were fought from 1881-1889. It also fought a war against its Irish subjects in the aftermath of World War I, which culminated in an independent Ireland in 1922. It later initiated war along with France and Israel against Egypt in 1956 over President Nasser's nationalization of the Suez Canal.

Democratic India conquered Goa in 1961 and the Kingdom of Sikkim in 1975. The Republic of Georgia initiated war with Russia and South Ossetia, although Georgia's democratic credentials are superior to those of Russia.[146] Popularly elected Hamas regularly initiates war against Israel, while the less popular Palestinian Authority remains at peace.

To be sure, numerous wars have also been initiated by non-democratic regimes: the Third Reich, North Korea, Iraq, Pakistan, Egypt, Syria, Jordan, China, the Soviet Union, Germany, etc. But experience teaches that spreading democracy does not necessarily make the United States safer from attack.

President Truman failed to explain how supporting free peoples resisting subjugation by armed minorities or outside pressures would make the United States more secure, freer, or wealthier, or even how he would distinguish between free peoples and non-free peoples. Take Greece and Turkey, the first beneficiaries of the Truman Doctrine. In 1947, neither country was a democracy featuring competing political parties, free and fair elections, a free press, and the rule of law.

AMERICAN EMPIRE: BEFORE THE FALL

In Greece, civil war raged between royalists and communists. The United States backed the royalist side, even though its democratic credentials were slim. Suppose the communists had prevailed. Greece might still have been a thorn in the side of the Soviet Union like Tito's Yugoslavia. Greece would probably have become an economic albatross for the USSR like its satellites in Central or Eastern Europe. Greece had no alluring national resources or economic assets to plunder. Its military was unimpressive. Greece joined the North Atlantic Treaty Organization in 1952, but never became a formidable military ally or strong economic partner. Its chronic disputes with Turkey are a headache for the United States. Repressive military rule prevailed in Greece from 1967-74, including an attempt to overthrow the Greek Cypriot government on Cyprus.

If President Truman had terminated his assistance to the Greek royalists, the United States could have used the savings to strengthen its defenses at home, for instance, building additional aircraft carriers or spy planes or thickening border security. In addition, the royalists might have confronted the Greek Communists with greater resolve if the United States had required them to defend by generating greater popular support through reforms. In sum, President Truman proffered not a crumb of evidence that saving Greece from communism mattered a bit to the national security of the United States. Hungary turned Communist in 1947, but no evidence had surfaced that the United States had been made less safe. Similarly, the Communist coup in Czechoslovakia in 1948 did not heighten danger to United States sovereignty.

Turkey, like Greece, was bereft of the trappings of democracy in 1947. The government had lifted a ban on opposition political parties only two years earlier. Martial law remained in force until December 1947. Individual freedoms were severely compromised under Turkey's constitution. Thus, assisting Turkey under the *Truman Doctrine* was not assisting an authentic democracy. Moreover, as with Greece, if Turkey fell to communists, the United States would not have been less safe, less free, or less wealthy. Turkey is virtually all Muslim, like Afghanistan or Central Asia.

Turks would have fiercely resisted "godless communism" and the Soviet Union irrespective of United States aid. The Ottoman Empire had regularly fought Russia for centuries before it was vivisected after World War I. Attempts to suppress Islam and Turkish nationalism would have bogged the USSR down in perpetuity. Turkey would have proven indigestible.

Similarly, Communism has been repudiated in Afghanistan both before and after the Soviet invasion in 1979. Afghanistan proved the sepulcher of the Soviet Empire. No predominantly Muslim nation has ever been ruled by communists for a non-trivial period. Indeed, Russia exercises an exiguous yet costly control over predominantly Muslim populations in Chechnya, Dagestan, and Ingushetia. And China's Muslim Uighur population despises the Chinese Communist Party.

When one of Turkey's neighbors—Romania—fell behind the Soviet Iron Curtain after World War II, the United States did not become less safe. No Romanian soldier ever killed or threatened to kill an American. None were recruited to become part of the Soviet Red Army. Further, the United States could have used the resources saved by declining to assist Turkey to upgrade its defensive posture in the air, on the oceans, and on the ground along its borders. As with Greece, President Truman was unable to explain how rescuing Turkey from a communist takeover would be relevant to defending the sovereignty of the United States or the liberties of its people.

There is a straight line between the Truman Doctrine and President George W. Bush's 2007 State of the Union Address sounding a national call to save the world from hunger, poverty, and disease:

> American foreign policy is more than a matter of war and diplomacy. Our work in the world is also based on a timeless truth: To whom much is given, much is required. We hear the call to take on the challenges of hunger and poverty and disease -- and that is precisely what America is doing.[147]

President Bush voiced even more utopian ambitions and crusading zeal in his Second Inaugural address to end tyranny on the planet and to bring liberty and self-government to every corner of the world as a matter of duty and national survival. He bettered the instruction of Truman, who was inhibited by a rival superpower poised to exploit American overreaching. President Bush preached:

> We are led, by events and common sense, to one conclusion: The survival of liberty in our land increasingly depends on the success of liberty in other lands. The best hope for peace in our world is the expansion of freedom in all the world.

> America's vital interests and our deepest beliefs are now one. From the day of our Founding, we have proclaimed that every man and woman on this earth has rights, and dignity, and matchless value, because they bear the image of the Maker of Heaven and earth. Across the generations we have proclaimed the imperative of self-government, because no one is fit to be a master, and no one deserves to be a slave. Advancing these ideals is the mission that created our Nation. It is the honorable achievement of our fathers. Now it is the urgent requirement of our nation's security, and the calling of our time.
> So it is the policy of the United States to seek and support the growth of democratic movements and institutions in every nation and culture, with the ultimate goal of ending tyranny in our world.[148]

TWIN MYTHS OF THE AMERICAN EMPIRE

The absurdities of Truman's tenets outlived the Cold War. President Bush's messianic conception of national purpose was echoed in President Obama's Nobel Peace Prize address where he maintained that the liberties and happiness of Americans depended on the United States bringing the same blessings to every person on the planet.

The first orthodoxy's fatuous insistence that international stability must be maintained to strengthen national security also informed the *Truman Doctrine*. President Truman sermonized:

> [W]e cannot allow changes in the status quo in violation of the Charter of the United Nations by such methods as coercion, or by such subterfuges as political infiltration. In helping free and independent nations to maintain their freedom, the United States will be giving effect to the principles of the Charter of the United Nations.[149]

But Truman neglected to explain why protecting the international status quo is beneficial to American security and prosperity. The United States has allowed numerous changes in violation of the United Nation's Charter with no impairment of its safety, freedom, or economic success. India absorbed Goa, Sikkim, and Kashmir by military means. It gave birth to Bangladesh in 1971. Indonesia conquered East Timor in 1975 (only to disgorge the territory in 1999). The Soviet Union intervened militarily in Hungary in 1956 and Czechoslovakia in 1969 to suppress internal dissent or rebellion. China invaded Tibet in 1950. The list of military alterations of the status quo in violation of the Charter without impact on United States sovereignty or national security is endless.

Furthermore, a nation expanding territorially through military aggression or otherwise ordinarily *reduces its threat* to American sovereignty. Military invasions routinely weaken the aggressor by squandering military and economic resources in occupying or controlling hostile populations. The Soviet Union's domination of Eastern and Central Europe during the Cold War until the fall of the Berlin Wall in 1989 is emblematic. During that approximately 40-year interval, the USSR encountered uprisings or serious resistance in East Germany (1953), Hungary (1956), Czechoslovakia (1968), and Poland (1970, 1976, and 1980). Romania charted an independent course under the despotic President Nikolai Ceausescu. Yugoslavia under Tito marched to its own drummer. The Soviet Union did not entrust its nuclear weapons to its Eastern and Central European satellites because their loyalties were suspect. They were an economic deadweight requiring billions in Soviet subsidies annually. They contributed nothing to the U.S.S.R.'s global military ambitions or profile—whether under the umbrella of the Warsaw Pact or otherwise. They did not send soldiers to fight in Afghanistan in 1979. They did not collaborate with the Red Army in its periodic clashes with China over the Ussuri River border. They did not send troops to assist Soviet forces in Angola, Somalia, Ethiopia, or otherwise. They did not contribute scientists to develop weapons of mass destruction.

Military conquests are ordinarily money losers because of the staggering expense of military occupation required to prevent sabotage and defeat insurgencies. The Nazi occupation of France in World War II weakened its capabilities. The British Empire was a drain on the British economy. The United States gained wealth by granting the Philippines independence in 1946, and would gain more if Puerto Rico opted for nationhood. The United States should rejoice at the imbecilic wars fought by foreign countries. Such wars weaken their ability to attack the United States. The Soviet Empire's invasion of Afghanistan in 1979, not Star Wars, was the sepulcher of the USSR.

Even if conquest augmented national power, the Brobdignagian military profile of the United States plus its staggering capacity to retaliate is sufficient to prevent any assault on United States sovereignty irrespective of developments abroad.

The Founding Fathers fiercely opposed foreign entanglements, which invariably undermine the Constitution's mission and philosophy.[150] The

United Nations Charter, a treaty ratified by the United States Senate, is persuasive evidence. In the name of defending international peace and security, Chapter VII of the Charter purports to empower the President to unilaterally enlist United States forces in warfare at the behest of the United Nations Security Council. Chapter VII's entrusting of the war power to an international body unaccountable to the United States is flagrantly unconstitutional.

The Supreme Court has held that certain legislative powers may not be delegated. It concluded in *Clinton v. New York* (1998) that Congress could not delegate its power over taxing and spending to the President via a line-item veto. The power of Congress to authorize the initiation of war is even more important than its power to tax and spend. It was the inarguable intent of the Constitution's architects to bestow this power exclusively upon Congress

The Korean War aptly illustrates the disastrous consequences of circumventing that clear intent. Before committing troops there, President Truman obtained a United Nations Security Council resolution authorizing military force against North Korea to rebuff its June 25, 1950 aggression against South Korea, an infraction which created no plausible danger to the United States. This occasioned the constitutionally unjustifiable deaths of 33,000 American soldiers.[151]

The Truman Doctrine's professed intent to assist free people in defending against foreign oppressors was routinely ignored in building an American Empire. Realpolitik eclipsed any concerns for democracy and human rights during the Cold War. American actions were motivated by opposition to the Soviet Empire and its retaliatory capabilities in lieu of promoting democracy or human rights at any cost. President Truman supported South Korea's President Syngman Rhee in the Korean War despite his autocratic ways. Rhee was later forced to resign in 1960 by popular protests over a rigged election.

The people of Eastern and Central Europe received no serious assistance from Truman in attempting to separate themselves from the system of Communist satellites in Central and Eastern Europe in contravention of the Yalta Accords. Germany and Berlin were divided. Czechoslovakia fell into the Communist orbit in 1948. Hungary had done the same one year earlier. Soon after, in 1950, Tibet lost its autonomy to Communist China. In none of these situations did the United States intervene militarily to prevent the coercion of free people.

President Dwight D. Eisenhower extended aid and military assistance to Spain's Dictator Francisco Franco in a package of 1953 Madrid Agreements, but did nothing to assist the Hungarians in their 1956 revolt against Soviet domination. He then attempted to overthrow the non-aligned and democratically elected Indonesian government in 1958 in favor of non-democratic forces. President John F. Kennedy supported despotism in South Vietnam by opposing Communist North Vietnam, but did nothing to halt the construction of the Berlin Wall and a Communist takeover of Laos. President Lyndon B. Johnson backed a non-democratic regime in the Dominican Republic, ostensibly to prevent a Communist or Socialist government coming to power, but passively watched as the Soviet Union put an end to Prague Spring. President Richard Nixon forged close ties with Nicaraguan strongman Anastasio Somoza, overthrew Chile's Salvador Allende in favor of military dictator Augustino Pinochet, and befriended Communist China at the expense of Taiwan. President Gerald Ford supported anti-Communist, racist regimes in South Africa and Rhodesia. President Jimmy Carter enthused over the Shah of Iran. And every President has been a staunch friend of Saudi Arabia because of its vast oil and gas supplies despite its despicable religious bigotry (which gave birth to Osama bin Laden and 9/11) and repulsive despotism. These examples, which could be endlessly augmented, demonstrate the moral emptiness of the *Truman Doctrine*. The Founding Fathers correctly viewed with suspicion any nation's claim that altruism or martyrdom would be as the North Star of its foreign policy.

The second specious orthodoxy, spawned as early as the Spanish American War, is that United States prosperity pivots on the maintenance of peace and stability abroad by projecting its military to secure trade routes and access to strategic economic resources. President

TWIN MYTHS OF THE AMERICAN EMPIRE

Eisenhower voiced the orthodoxy in speaking at New Orleans on October 7, 1953:

> For today our whole economy turns and depends upon the commerce of the world through such ports as [New Orleans]...This dependence of our industry is certain to increase as the tempo of our industry increases. It highlights the most compelling practical reason why we must have friends in the world. We know that nations of hostile intent would not trade with us except as it suited their own convenience. And this means that hostile rule of areas supplying us essential imports would place the American production line at the mercy of those who hope for its destruction.

> But foreign trade means much more than the obtaining of vital raw materials from other nations. It means effectively strengthening our friends in the world at large – strengthening them not only to fortify their own economies – not only to be independent of direct financial aid from wealthier nations – but also to buy from us what we must sell to the world.

> By making it possible for our friends to sell their products to us, we thus at once help them to be strong and enable them to earn the dollars by which they can, in turn help our economy to be healthy and progressive. Clearly, we need these friends abroad, just as they need us.[152]

At another venue, Eisenhower amplified:

From my viewpoint, foreign policy is, or should be, based primarily upon one consideration. That consideration is the need for the U.S. to obtain certain raw materials to sustain its economy and, when possible, to preserve profitable foreign markets for our surpluses. Out of this need grows the necessity for making certain that those areas of the world in which essential raw materials are produced are not only accessible to us, but their populations and governments are willing to trade with us on a friendly basis.[153]

The second orthodoxy encouraged the United States to establish hundreds of military bases abroad and to deploy a formidable Blue Water Navy.

But neither the United States nor any other country has ever been denied access to strategic materials or trade by so-called "enemies." Smuggling, bribery, or middlemen eager to make money invariably evade the tightest embargoes. The Soviet Union effortlessly outfoxed the United States wheat embargo following its invasion of Afghanistan in 1979 by purchasing greater quantities from middlemen like Spain or Argentina. The penurious North Korea, with its millions of starving citizens, remains defiant in the face of massive international embargoes. Fidel Castro's Cuba has circumvented more than 50 years of a United States embargo. Despite the expenditure of $44 billion dollars annually and the employment of the world's most proficient military and law enforcement assets, the United States has been unable to dent the flow of narcotics flooding across its borders to satisfy millions of American consumers.[154]

The October 1973 oil embargo imposed by the Organization of the Petroleum Exporting Countries (OPEC) failed. Oil supplies were tight before the embargo was imposed. Shortages were caused by President Nixon's price controls and the curtailment of gasoline to independent service stations amidst climbing crude prices. By May 1973, 1,000 service stations had closed for lack of fuel, five months before the OPEC embargo.[155] Countries exempt from the embargo hiked purchases from OPEC members for resale to the United States. Even the Saudi oil minister Sheik Yamani acknowledged that the embargo "did not imply that we could reduce imports to the United States…the world is really just one market. So the embargo was more symbolic than anything else."[156] Former United States Secretary of State Henry Kissinger concurred: "In fact, the Arab embargo was a symbolic gesture of limited practical importance."[157] Even OPEC's promise to cut oil production was short lived, as they ordered a 10 percent production increase in January 1974, effectively ending the alleged crisis. In contrast, the United States economy was thrown into a tailspin following the rocketing of crude oil prices in 2008 with no embargos or wars.

Rabidly anti-American regimes eagerly trade with the United States. Venezuelan President Hugo Chavez maligns the United States as "the great Satan" and the enemy of Venezuela.[158] But Venezuela maintains extensive commercial ties with the United States. It is one of the largest Latin American investors, and one of America's top four foreign oil suppliers.[159] Bilateral trade between the two countries totaled $50 billion in 2007.[160] Iran, archenemy of the United States, increased American imports tenfold during President George W. Bush's presidency.[161] Iran would sell oil to the United States if the legal prohibition were lifted.

International instability has historically bolstered rather than depressed the United States economy. During World War I, trade between the U.S. and Europe exploded long before a single American soldier stepped foot on French soil. Between 1911 and 1916, trade with Italy jumped from $107,519,515 to $363,765,648; with France from $250,068,348 to $969,714,125; and with the United Kingdom from $788,932,491 to a total of $2,192,867,617. United States trade with Europe more than doubled between 1911 and 1916, from $2,063,466,098 to $4,446,595,210 amidst war raging across the continent.[162]

In the run-up to Pearl Harbor, United States trade with Europe steadily expanded from an average of $959,989 in 1931-1935 to $1,332,087 in 1936-1940, $1,643,174 in 1940, and $1,840,052 in 1941. Asian trade saw a similar spike, despite the persistence of Japanese aggression from 1937 to the end of the war. American trade with Asia rose from an annual average of $349,911 in 1931-1935 to an annual average of $535,283 in 1936-1940; $619,210 in 1940; and $625,198 in 1941.[163] Again, this rise in American wealth occurred before a single U.S. soldier engaged in hostilities and during an era of unparalleled international convulsions. This stunning prosperity derived from global turmoil occurred despite the termination of trade with Austria-Hungary and Germany during World War I and Nazi Germany and Japan in World War II, all key trading partners to the U.S. prior to the commencement of hostilities. In sum, international strife is generally a fillip for the American economy.

In any event, the United States economy is not dependent on international trade.[164] American exports represented 13.1% of the U.S. GDP - $14.26 trillion – in 2008.[165] Of that 13.1%, or $1.86 trillion, 17.6% of exports went to Canada, 12.0% to China, 10.8% to Mexico, 6.1% to Japan, 4.5% to Germany, and 3.3% to the United Kingdom.[166] Other states collectively received less than 3% of American exports. All figures are comparable to prior years. Payments from these six states constituted 7.1% of the American GDP, with Canada, China, and Mexico contributing the lion's share.

South Korea receives 2.4% of U.S. exports, representing only 0.3% of the U.S. GDP. The tens of thousands of United States soldiers stationed there are superfluous to the health of the United States economy.

Despite their patent falsity, the orthodoxies of democracy, international stability, and economic security are customarily invoked by the American Empire to justify its global military projection, endless and omnipresent wars, and national security state.

Corresponding lies or myths were contrived by the Roman Empire to the same ends. Joseph Schumpeter's 1919 essay, "The Sociology of Imperialism" recounted:

There was no corner of the world where some interest was not alleged to be in danger or under actual attack. If the interests were not Roman, they were of Rome's allies; and if Rome had no allies, then allies would be invented. When it was utterly impossible to contrive such an interest- then it was the national honor that had been insulted. The fight was always invested with an aura of legality. Rome was always being attacked by evil-minded neighbors, always fighting for a breathing space. The whole world was pervaded by a host of enemies, and it was manifestly Rome's duty to guard against their indubitably aggressive designs.[167]

6

Crucifying The Rule Of Law On
A National Security Cross

In times of war, the Constitution's checks and balances are crippled. Secrecy trumps transparency. Legal transgressions escape prosecution and punishment in the name of national security. The American Empire's lawlessness in commencing war is emblematic of its general profanation of the rule of law.

On June 25, 1950, North Korea launched a vicious military campaign against their southern neighbor aimed at uniting the two Korean states under communist rule. The newly created United Nations condemned North Korea's aggression as "a breach of the peace," called for it to withdraw its invading forces, and requested all UN member states to "render every assistance" to the multilateral organization in the enforcement of the UN resolution. Before consulting with congressional leaders, President Harry Truman committed American naval and air forces to the defense of South Korea. Truman invoked the United Nations resolution as authorization.

On June 29th, Truman characterized what he had done as Commander in Chief as part of a "police action" during a presidential news conference. A reporter asked, "Mr. President, everybody is asking in this country, are we or are we not at war."[168] Truman replied with a simple declaration: "We are not at war." Another reporter asked the president, "Would it be correct, against your explanation, to call this a police action under the United Nations?" "Yes," Truman replied. "That is exactly what it amounts to."[169] Hours after Truman made his "police action" statement on June 29th, he ordered a contingent of American ground troops into South Korea, bolstering their numbers a day later. Two weeks after the first utterance of a "police action" in Korea at the president's July 13 news conference, a reporter asked: "Do you still call this a police action?" Truman replied in the affirmative, but transformed the word "action" to "reaction": "Yes," he said, "it is still a police reaction."[170] Truman made this comment despite the fact that the USS *Juneau* had destroyed North Korean torpedo boats near Chumunjin, US aircraft from the USS *Valley Forge* had hit North Korean airfields, and the 34th Infantry Regiment (24th Division) had fought a two-day engagement with communist troops at Osan between June 29th and his July 13th news conference.[171]

Truman deceived Congress and the American public by fatuously characterizing the Korean War as a "police action" to obviate the need for a constitutionally required congressional declaration of war. He feared Congress would balk at dispatching conscripted United States soldiers abroad to risk that last full measure of devotion for South Koreans with no loyalty or obligations to the United States. According to his biographer, David McCulloch, Truman fretted that an "appeal to Congress now would make it more difficult for future presidents to deal with emergencies [by circumventing the Constitution]."[172]

On June 29, 1950, Secretary of State Dean Acheson claimed that all U.S. actions taken in Korea "have been under the aegis of the United Nations." But the President is sworn to uphold and to defend the Constitution of the United States, not the United Nations Charter or other treaties that may contradict constitutional stipulations. The Supreme Court explained in *Reid v. Covert, 354 U.S. 1* (1957):

CRUCIFYING THE RULE OF LAW

Article VI, the Supremacy Clause of the Constitution, declares:

"This Constitution, and the Laws of the United States which shall be made in Pursuance thereof, and all Treaties made, or which shall be made, under the Authority of the United States, shall be the supreme Law of the Land . ..".

There is nothing in this language which intimates that treaties and laws enacted pursuant to them may flout the Constitution. Nor is there anything in the debates which accompanied the drafting and ratification of the Constitution which even suggests such a result. These debates, as well as the history that surrounds the adoption of the treaty provision in Article VI, make it clear that the reason treaties were not limited to those made in "pursuance" of the Constitution was so that agreements made by the United States under the Articles of Confederation, including the important peace treaties which concluded the Revolutionary War, would remain in effect. It would be manifestly contrary to the objectives of those who created the Constitution, as well as those who were responsible for the Bill of Rights—let alone alien to our entire constitutional history and tradition—to construe Article VI as permitting the United States to exercise power under an international agreement without observing constitutional prohibitions. In effect, such construction would permit amendment of that document in a manner not sanctioned by Article V. The prohibitions of the Constitution were designed to apply to all branches of the National Government, and they cannot be nullified by the Executive or by the Executive and the Senate combined.

In other words, the United Nations Charter Treaty would be unconstitutional if it empowered the President to employ the United States military in war without congressional authorization.

Secretary Acheson's State Department attempted to legitimize Truman's unconstitutional decision by releasing a memorandum listing 87 instances in which presidents had unilaterally sent American forces into combat.[173] The constitutional theory was that "the President, as Commander in Chief of the Armed Forces of the United States, has full control over the use thereof," that there was a "traditional power of the President to use the armed forces of the United States without consulting Congress," and that this had often been done in "the broad interests of American foreign policy."[174] Senator Paul Douglas, liberal Democrat, supported Truman's euphemistically styled "police action." Summoning United Nations resolutions, the liberal Senator pleaded that the deployment of military force to drive North Korea back to the 38th parallel "was not an act of war, but, instead, merely the exercise of police power under international sanction."[175]

The precedents summoned by Acheson, the State Department, and Douglas were unconvincing because they were confined to suppressing piracy—a universal crime-or protecting American lives or property abroad. Scholar Louis Fisher described them as mostly "fights with pirates, landings of small naval contingents on barbarous or semi-barbarous coasts, the dispatch of small bodies of troops to chase bandits or cattle rustlers across the Mexico border, and the like."[176]

The State Department's examples were not precedents for sustained major wars against sovereign states. If they were, *the whole reason for fastening responsibility for war on Congress in the Constitution would have been undone, i.e. distrust of the President's institutional inclination to make war to aggrandize his own powers at the expense of coequal branches of government, individual liberty, and transparency.*

Louis Fisher has thoroughly discredited the constitutional arguments of Truman and Acheson. He has written that nothing in the history of the UN Charter suggests Congress had even attempted to surrender its war powers. It was drafted with knowledge that America's entry into the League of Nations had stumbled when President Wilson and the Senate clashed over the Treaty of Versailles. Wilson refused to accept reservations offered by Senator Henry Cabot Lodge designed to protect the congressional prerogative to authorize the initiation of war.

The Senate debated the UN Charter on July 27, 1945. President Truman wired a note from Potsdam to Senator Kenneth McKeller to acknowledge his obligation to obtain congressional approval for war if he concluded special agreements with the Security Council to contribute armed forces or other military assistance to execute a Council resolution: "When any such agreement or agreements are negotiated it will be my purpose to ask the Congress for appropriate legislation to approve them."[177] With that understanding, the Senate approved the UN Charter, voting 89 to 2.

The United Nations Participation Act of 1945 is to the same effect. It provides that all UN special agreements for the use of United States troops "shall be subject to the approval of the Congress by appropriate Act or joint resolution."[178] Congress did not engraft any exceptions because it did not wield the constitutional power to do so. The Founding Fathers believed only Congress could be trusted to decide whether the lives and liberties of citizens should be risked by beginning war because a legal state of belligerency diminishes rather than enlarges congressional powers.

President Truman maintained at a press conference that presidential authority to dispatch troops abroad absent a congressional directive had been "repeatedly recognized by the Congress and court."[179] Although ignorant of case law, Truman asserted that, "you will find decisions by at least three Chief Justices on that very subject."[180] The decisions were figments of the President's imagination. The Supreme Court expressly declared that only Congress is empowered to initiate war against a foreign nation in the *Prize Cases.*

Justice Robert Jackson emphasized the lawlessness of the Korean War and its invitation to unchecked presidential emergency powers in a prescient concurring opinion in *Youngstown Sheet & Tube v. Sawyer* (1952). There, the Court held unconstitutional President Truman's unilateral seizure of a private steel mill as Commander in Chief to prevent a strike that could have hampered the production of war material. Justice Jackson responded to the President's argument that he was empowered to fight wars without congressional authorization or support:

> That seems to be the logic of an argument tendered at our bar—that the President having, on his own responsibility, sent American troops abroad derives from that act "affirmative power" to seize the means of producing a supply of steel for them. To quote,

> "Perhaps the most forceful illustration of the scope of Presidential power in this connection is the fact that American troops in Korea, whose safety and effectiveness are so directly involved here, were sent to the field by an exercise of the President's constitutional powers."

Thus, it is said, he has invested himself with "war powers." I cannot foresee all that it might entail if the Court should indorse this argument. Nothing in our Constitution is plainer than that declaration of a war is entrusted only to Congress. Of course, a state of war may, in fact, exist without a formal declaration. But no doctrine that the Court could promulgate would seem to me more sinister and alarming than that a President whose conduct of foreign affairs is so largely uncontrolled, and often even is unknown, can vastly enlarge his mastery over the internal affairs of the country by his own commitment of the Nation's armed forces to some foreign venture. I do not, however, find it necessary or appropriate to consider the legal status of the Korean enterprise to discountenance argument based on it.

Assuming that we are in a war *de facto*, whether it is or is not a war *de jure*, does that empower the Commander in Chief to seize industries he thinks necessary to supply our army? The Constitution expressly places in Congress power "to raise and **support** Armies" and "to **provide** and **maintain** a Navy." (Emphasis supplied.) This certainly lays upon Congress primary responsibility for supplying the armed forces. Congress alone controls the raising of revenues and their appropriation, and may determine in what manner and by what means they shall be spent for military and naval procurement. I suppose no one would doubt that Congress can take over war supply as a Government enterprise."

Yet Jackson foresaw that nothing the Court did would forestall presidential usurpations if Congress neglected to defend its constitutional turf:

But I have no illusion that any decision by this Court can keep power in the hands of Congress if it is not wise and timely in meeting its problems. A crisis that challenges the President equally, or perhaps primarily, challenges Congress. If not good law, there was worldly wisdom in the maxim attributed to Napoleon that "The tools belong to the man who can use them." We may say that power to legislate for emergencies belongs in the hands of Congress, but only Congress itself can prevent power from slipping through its fingers.

The essence of our free Government is "leave to live by no man's leave, underneath the law"—to be governed by those impersonal forces which we call law. Our Government is fashioned to fulfill this concept so far as humanly possible. The Executive, except for recommendation and veto, has no legislative power. The executive action we have here originates in the individual will of the President, and represents **an exercise of authority without law [emphasis added]**. No one, perhaps not even the President, knows the limits of the power he may seek to exert in this instance, and the parties affected cannot learn the limit of their rights. We do not know today what powers over labor or property would be claimed to flow from Government possession if we should legalize it, what rights to compensation would be claimed or recognized, or on what contingency it would end. With all its defects, delays and inconveniences, men have discovered no technique for long preserving free government except that the Executive be under the law, and that the law be made by parliamentary deliberations.

Such institutions may be destined to pass away. But it is the duty of the Court to be last, not first, to give them up.

The Korean War was flagrantly unconstitutional. The presidential-congressional-judicial dialogue on that score is conclusive. Yet neither Congress nor the American people protested. The American Empire's political culture excused a multitude of constitutional sins.

To jump chronologically from Korea to Iraq in 2003, a lawsuit was initiated challenging the constitutionality of the congressional delegation of authority to President George W. Bush to decide whether to commence war against Iraq in *John Doe I et al v. President George W. Bush, et al.* The lawsuit was dismissed by the United States Court of Appeals for the First Circuit for reasons unrelated to the merits of the non-delegation claim.

The American Empire mindlessly accepts presidential lawlessness in initiating war as de facto constitutional. Before the invasion of Iraq in March 2003, when a reporter questioned President Bush about initiating war, he snapped: "I'm the person who gets to decide, not you."[181] The exclusive power of Congress was ignored in both the question and answer. Similarly, no rival candidate or member of the media raised eyebrows over Hillary Clinton's statement during her 2008 presidential campaign that she would unilaterally obliterate Iran if it attacked Israel. The same is true for President Obama's Nobel Peace Prize remarks asserting unilateral presidential power to initiate war to defend the United States whenever the president discerns a foreign threat from either a state or non-state actor. Those remarks also asserted that President Obama had unilaterally made torture illegal, although its illegality rests on a federal statute and treaty.

Lawlessness in the name of national security would be partially excusable if the American people benefited. But they have not. Truman's unconstitutional war in Korea occasioned over 33,000 Americans killed in action and more than 136,000 casualties on the Korean peninsula and enormous budgetary expenditures.[182] There was no corresponding benefit to defending United States sovereignty, the United States Constitution, or the liberties of the American people.

Suppose the United States had idled while communist North Korea, assisted by China and the Soviet Union, attacked and defeated autocratic South Korea. The United States would not have been less safe. It could have re-deployed its Korean War resources to the United States to construct improved missile defenses and spy planes and to fortify the nation's borders. North Korea would not have attacked the United States mainland or possessions. Both the capability and motivation were lacking. It has never displayed imperial ambitions to cross the Pacific Ocean. North Korea required the massive intervention of Communist Chinese troops to avoid defeat. An attack on the United States would have invited North Korea's incineration.

A North Korean conquest of the South would have embroiled the North Korean Army and security services in endless strife with the more educated and advanced South Koreans. Those internal convulsions would further have inhibited any North Korean adventurism against the United States. Its economic interests would likewise have been undisturbed. United States trade with South Korea is but a tiny fraction of its gross national product. Further, United States trade with an all-Communist Korea might have thrived as it has with Communist China and Vietnam. Finally, it is doubtful that North Korea would have acquired nuclear weapons and developed advanced missile systems if the United States had resisted entering the Korean conflict. The North's nuclear ambitions have been fueled by fear that the United States intends to overthrow the regime by force, violence, or infiltration. That apprehension is compounded by the presence of a United States military base in South Korea hosting tens of thousands of United States soldiers coupled with the American Empire's credo of military intervention for professed humanitarian causes.

The Vietnam War, like the Korean War, was an unconstitutional disaster. Tens of thousands of American soldiers were killed. Hundreds of thousands were wounded. Large numbers were afflicted with dioxin-related diseases. Napalm denuded the countryside. Women and children were slain at My Lai. Prisoners were held in tiger cages. Congress and the American people were deceived over the secret bombing of Cambodia. Hundreds of billions of dollars were squandered on a fool's errand. More bombs were dropped on the Ho Chi Minh trail than in all of World War II without result.

President Lyndon B. Johnson deceived Congress and the American people over twin "Gulf of Tonkin" incidents—a high crime and misdemeanor that would have justified the President's impeachment and removal from office under Article II, section 4 of the Constitution. The deception convinced Congress to pass the Gulf of Tonkin Resolution of August 10, 1964 by a unanimous vote in the House and an 88-2 vote in the Senate. It unconstitutionally delegated to the President the decision to commence war against North Vietnam to protect South Vietnamese citizens with no allegiance or obligations to the United States.

North Vietnamese warships allegedly attacked American vessels thousands of miles away from American shores on August 2nd and August 4th of 1964. In an address to the American public on the latter date, President Johnson exaggerated the ostensible danger from North Vietnam manifold to justify war and aggrandize power:

> The initial attack on the destroyer Maddox, on August 2,
> was repeated today by a number of hostile vessels attacking
> two U.S. destroyers with torpedoes. The destroyers and
> supporting aircraft acted at once on the orders I gave after

the initial act of aggression...In the larger sense this new act of aggression, aimed directly at our own forces, again brings home to all of us in the United States the importance of the struggle for peace and security in Southeast Asia. Aggression by terror against the peaceful villagers of South Viet-Nam has now been joined by open aggression on the high seas against the United States of America.[183]

In a speech to Congress on August 5th 1964, Johnson amplified:

Last night I announced to the American people that the North Vietnamese regime had conducted further deliberate attacks against U.S. naval vessels operating in international waters, and that I had therefore directed air action against gun boats and supporting facilities used in these hostile operations...These latest actions of the North Vietnamese regime have given new and grave turn to the already serious situation in southeast Asia.[184]

President Johnson's assertion that the attacks were unprovoked was ludicrous. His comments concealed that he had initiated a clandestine program of coastal and air raids against North Vietnamese targets, known as OPLAN 34A, on February 1, 1964, and was using the *Maddox* and other specialty vessels to collect intelligence during the operations and identify North Vietnamese military targets. On June 30th, 1964, South Vietnamese commandoes staged a large amphibious assault on the communist islands Hon Me and Hon Nieu, with the USS *Maddox* monitoring the assault from 120 miles away. On the following night, the island of Hon Me was shelled, presumably as part of the OPLAN 34A operations, with the *Maddox* in close proximity. The intelligence the *Maddox* collected was likely utilized to coordinate and launch further covert operations, according to some histo-rians.[185] The American warship was also present during a South Vietnamese raid just before the infamous attack on August 2nd. That attack was provoked by the United States, contrary to President Johnson's prevarications.

Johnson also withheld that even his Secretary of Defense agreed that he had deceived the American people about August 2, and, further, that there were conflicting reports on whether or not the second Gulf of Tonkin incident ever took place. It did not. Consider the following seg-ments of an August 3rd 1964 discussion between Robert McNamara and President Johnson regarding the first attack:

> Robert McNamara: "…And I think I should also, or we should also at that time, Mr. President, explain this OPLAN 34-A, these covert operations. There's no question but what that had bearing on it. On Friday night, as you probably know, we had four TP [sic] boats from [South] Vietnam, manned by [South] Vietnamese or other nationals, attack two islands, and we expend-ed, oh, 1,000 rounds of ammunition of one kind or an-other against them. We probably shot up a radar station and a few other miscellaneous buildings. And following 24 hours after that with this destroyer in that same area undoubtedly led them to connect the two events…"[186]

> President Johnson: "Ok. Here's what we did: We [were] within their 12-mile [territorial waters] limit, and that's a matter that hasn't been settled. But there have been some covert operations in that area that we have been carrying on — blowing up some bridges and things of that kind, roads and so forth. So I imagine they wanted to put a stop to it. So they come out there and fire and

we respond immediately with five-inch guns from the destroyer and with planes overhead.[187]

After the Secretary of Defense received a report on the second attack on US ships, which prompted the President to retaliate with air raids, Captain Herrick, commander of the *Maddox,* immediately sent another report that read: "Review of action makes many reported contacts and torpedoes fired appear doubtful. Freak weather effects on radar and over-eager sonarmen may have accounted for many reports. No actual visual sightings by Maddox. Suggest complete evaluation before any further action taken."[188]

By 1965, President Johnson admitted that the second attack on US naval warships may have been imaginary: "For all I know, our navy was shooting at whales out there."[189]

To deceive Congress and the American people to obtain authorization for war is an impeachable offense justifying the President's removal from office. James Iredell, during North Carolina's ratification debates over the Constitution, explained:

> The President must certainly be punishable for giving false information to the Senate. He is to regulate all intercourse with foreign powers, and it is his duty to impart to the Senate every material intelligence he receives. If it should appear that he has not given them full information, but has concealed important intelligence which he ought to have communicated, and by that means induced them to enter into measures injurious to their country, and which they would not have consented to had the true state of things been disclosed to them—in this case, I ask whether, upon an impeach-

> ment for a misdemeanor upon such an account, the
> Senate would probably favor him. [190]

The Vietnam War was not only unconstitutional. It was folly. No national security interest of the United States was implicated. When Indochina (Vietnam, Cambodia, and Laos) fell into the Communist orbit in 1975, the safety and security of the United States remained unimpaired. Communist China soon attacked Communist Vietnam in 1979. And Communist Vietnam soon attacked Communist Cambodia under Pol Pot in 1979. Russia abandoned its naval base at Cam Ranh Bay in 2002 because the rent was prohibitive. The United States lost more than 55,000 courageous soldiers in Vietnam to propitiate the puerile craving of the American Empire to dominate the world for the sake of domination.

The United States professed ambition to export democracy to South Vietnam encroached on the domain of farce. President Kennedy endorsed the overthrow of South Vietnamese President Ngo Dinh Diem in 1963 by the South Vietnamese military to promote a legitimate government devoted to the rule of law. But Diem was assassinated. A legitimate South Vietnamese government never arrived. South Vietnam was ruled by a succession of undistinguished military figures until its conquest by North Vietnam in 1975: General Duong Van Minh, General Nguyen Cao Ky, and General Nguyen Van Thieu. Corruption was rife, and the grim visage of war was the Con Son Tiger Cages.

President Johnson's unilateral and unconstitutional military intervention in the Dominican Republic in April 1965 was predictably premised on false claims that the ongoing violence between the government and rebel forces threatened American lives, and that Cuba's Fidel Castro was threatening to install a Communist dupe in power. On April 28, 1965, President Johnson maintained:

> The United States Government has been informed by military authorities in the Dominican Republic that American lives are in danger...I have ordered the Secretary of Defense to put the necessary American troops ashore in order to give protection to hundreds of Americans who are still in the Dominican Republic and to escort them safely back to this country...[191]

He later stated on May 3rd that Ambassador Bennett was the catalyst behind the intervention, after he sent an urgent cable stating: "You must land troops immediately, or blood will run in the streets, American blood will run in the streets."[192]

President Johnson greatly exaggerated, if not totally fabricated, this threat to American lives to justify military intervention. His genuine objective was to prevent the defeat of a pro-US, anti-communist government in the Dominican Republic. Undersecretary Thomas Mann later admitted to the Senate Foreign Relations Committee: "We did instruct our Ambassador to go back to [pro-government Colonel] Benoit...and in order to improve our juridical base asked him to specifically say that he could not protect the lives of American citizens." As a result, Ambassador Bennett insisted that the large number of Americans residing at the Hotel Embajador were in danger of being killed or wounded, thus providing a justification for the intervention.[193]

Two days after marines entered the country, President Johnson stated that the mission was now not to simply protect American lives, but to also protect the sovereignty of the Dominican Republic and prevent a communist takeover. He told Senate Majority Leader Mike Mansfield: "The Castro forces are really gaining control...The big question is, Do we let Castro take over and us move out?"[194] In a May 2nd speech, President Johnson elaborated:

> Our forces, American forces, were ordered in immediately to protect American lives. They have done that... The revolutionary movement took a tragic turn. Communist leaders, many of them trained in Cuba... joined the revolution. They took increasing control. What began as a popular democratic revolution committed to democracy and social justice very shortly moved and was taken over and really seized and placed into the hands of a band of Communist conspirators.[195]

He also declared: "The American nation, cannot, must not, and will not, permit the establishment of another communist government in the western hemisphere."[196]

The President claimed that Cuba and communist conspirators were controlling the rebellion even though his Secretary of Defense warned on April 30th that the CIA had not "shown any evidence that I've seen that Castro has been directing this..."[197] A CIA cable to Washington on April 25th further reported that the Communist Party (Partido Socialista Dominicano) had been "unaware of the coup attempt."[198] In fact, when President Johnson instructed the CIA to provide evidence of communist involvement in the rebellion after the initial marine landing, no such evidence could be discovered. The President would later rely on J. Edgar Hoover to deploy FBI agents in the Dominican Republic to provide the names of 53 communist "conspirators." But 53 individuals are insufficient to persuade a rebel fighting force numbering tens of thousands. Further, many of the 53 identified by Hoover were out of the country or imprisoned.[199]

Honesty is the coin of any democratic realm to make political discourse meaningful. If the truth about the Dominican Republic were known to Congress, a bill would have been enacted prohibiting the expenditure of any funds of the United States to dispatch the armed forces there. Did President Johnson remember the staged origins of World War II? Early in August, 1939, a plan was conceived by the Chief of the Security

Police and SD Reinhard Heydrich, to stage simulated border raids by personnel of the GESTAPO and SD dressed as Poles. To add authenticity, Germany planned to take certain prisoners from concentration camps, kill them by use of hypodermic injections, and leave their bodies, clad in Polish uniforms, at the various places where the incidents were planned to occur. The Chief of the GESTAPO, Heinrich Muller, took a directing hand in these actions, which were staged on 31 August 1939 in Beuthen, Hindenburg, Gleiwitz, and elsewhere.

After World War II, United States national security experts advised that tactics of the enemy, i.e., world communism, must be employed to avoid defeat. President Johnson accepted that false precept in fashioning his national security policies. His presidency set the stage for the complete ruination of the American Republic.

The Dominican Republic military intervention furthered no constitutional objective. It neither bolstered the common defense nor secured the blessings of liberty for the American people. Suppose a disciple of Castro had come to power there. The Dominican Republic is but an impoverished inkblot on the world stage, like Haiti. Both are irrelevant to the destiny of the United States. At worst, the twin island nations irritate by facilitating illegal immigration or drug trafficking. President Johnson acted to protect a "sphere of influence" over neighboring countries to prevent their falling into a Communist orbit. Russia, following the footsteps of its imperial predecessor, the Soviet Union, similarly demands a "sphere of influence" along its borders, for example, with Georgia, Ukraine, or the Baltic States, among others. But Russia's claim has been which has been vocally protested by the United States, which reflects the double standards, which earmark all Empires. To borrow from *Animal Farm,* the American Empire professes that all nations are equal, but that some or more equal than are others.

President Nixon deceived the American public, Congress, and even other members of the executive branch to secretly bomb Cambodia in 1969. Congress would have denied funds to conduct the bombing if it had known the truth. The massive deception was an impeachable offense.

President Nixon dispatched a cable to the US ambassador to South Vietnam, Ellsworth Bunker, avowing that all plans regarding the possible bombing of North Vietnamese targets in Cambodia were suspended. He simultaneously ordered the commander of American forces in Vietnam, General Creighton W. Abrams, to plan for such a bombing campaign.[200] Through backchannels and a reliance on a few trustworthy military leaders, the President then ordered specific pilots in South Vietnam to abort their current missions during flight and had them redirected to specific coordinates in Cambodia. After they bombed the location, they would return to their bases and report that they had attacked targets in South Vietnam. Nixon then implemented a dual reporting system, ordering the Joint Chiefs of Staff to maintain two sets of records, with the false records being submitted to the United States Congress to deceive congressional leaders of any US attacks on Cambodia.[201] The veil of secrecy was so complete, at least temporarily, that even the Secretary of the Air Force was unaware of its existence.[202]

During the fourteen month campaign, 1969-1970, the Defense Department routinely falsified the classified bombing reports that it sent to the Senate Armed Services Committee. When the Senate Foreign Relations Committee held a secret session and asked Secretary of State William P. Rogers to discuss the relationship between the U.S. and Cambodia, Secretary Rogers furthered the administration's deceit, replying: "Cambodia is one country where we can say with complete assurance that our hands are clean and our hearts are pure."[203]

After disappointing results with the secret bombing campaign, President Nixon lied to the American public when he assured his fellow citizens that the United States had not previously "moved against these enemy sanctuaries [in Cambodia] because we did not wish to violate the territory of a neutral nation."[204] Nixon later attempted to rationalize his secrecy and lies in his memoirs: "Another reason for secrecy was the problem of domestic antiwar protest. My administration was only two months old, and I wanted to provoke as little public outcry as possible at the outset."

CRUCIFYING THE RULE OF LAW

Presidential lies for the purpose of shielding the White House from public wrath or discontent and thwarting government by the intelligent consent of the governed are hallmarks of Empire and lawlessness. National security claims trump the fundamental constitutional principles of separation of powers, government transparency, congressional war prerogatives, and a President who must abide by law, not flout it. Throughout Operation Menu, half a million tons of ordnance were dropped on a neutral country, with 3,875 sorties completed without congressional knowledge.[205] It accomplished none of its anti-Communist purposes. Cambodia soon succumbed to the homicidal Pol Pot, and South Vietnam fell to the North.

On November 27, 1995, President Clinton misled Congress and the American public by grossly exaggerating the relevance of Bosnia to the sovereignty or security of the United States to justify military intervention on his say-so:

> ...Let me say at the outset America's role will not be about fighting a war. It will be about helping the people of Bosnia to secure their own peace agreement. Our mission will be limited, focused, and under the command of an American general.

> In fulfilling this mission, we will have the chance to help stop the killing of innocent civilians, especially children, and at the same time, to bring stability to central Europe, a region of the world that is vital to our national interests. It is the right thing to do...

> Securing peace in Bosnia will also help to build a free and stable Europe. Bosnia lies at the very heart of Europe, next door to many of its fragile new democracies and

some of our closest allies. Generations of Americans have understood that Europe's freedom and Europe's stability is vital to our own national security. That's why we fought two wars in Europe,; that's why we launched the Marshall Plan to restore Europe; that's why we created NATO and waged the Cold War, and that's why we must help the nations of Europe to end their worst nightmare since World War II now...

If we're not there, NATO will not be there. The peace will collapse; the war will reignite; the slaughter of innocents will begin again. A conflict that already has claimed so many victims could spread like poison throughout the region, eat away at Europe's stability and erode our partnership with our European allies...[206]

President Clinton's designation of Bosnia as critical to European freedom and United States security was ludicrous. Congress refused to authorize use of the United States armed forces in Bosnia. President Clinton completely ignored their decision, defying his constitutional responsibility. His Secretary of State Madeleine Albright perfectly captured the psychology of Empire in quipping to Colin Powell, Chairman of the Joint Chiefs of Staff, "What's the point of having this superb military you're always talking about if we can't use it?"

Bosnia was no more likely to trigger a European conflagration like Sarajevo in August 1914 than was Georgia or Moldova. Both of the latter also confronted bloody internal insurgencies without infecting neighboring countries. At present, Bosnia is de facto partitioned between a rump state for Serbs and a rump state for Croats and Muslims, although the whole purpose of the military intervention was to prevent partition along ethnic or religious lines. Fifteen years after the Dayton Peace

Accords, Bosnia remains politically convulsed, occupied by American and other foreign troops, and governed by a European-backed Office of High Representative.

President Bush deceived both the American public and congressional leaders to garner support for the Iraq War, an impeachable offense. One fabrication was the supposed link between Al Qaeda and Iraq. President Bush falsely asserted on October 7, 2001:

> We know that Iraq and Al Qaeda have had high-level contacts that go back a decade...We've learned that Iraq has trained Al Qaeda members in bomb-making and poisons and deadly gases...Some citizens wonder, 'after 11 years of living with this [Saddam Hussein] problem, why do we need to confront it now?' And there's a reason. We have experienced the horror of September the 11th.[207]

Many executive branch officials compounded the falsehood. National Security adviser Condoleezza Rice maintained on September 25 2002, "There clearly are contacts between Al Qaeda and Iraq that can be documented; there clearly is testimony that some of the contacts have been important contacts and that there's a relationship there."[208] Two days later, Secretary of Defense Donald Rumsfeld stated that the CIA provided "bulletproof" evidence demonstrating "that there are in fact Al Qaeda in Iraq."[209] These statements were made despite the FBI's and CIA's strong doubts of any link. President Bush admitted on September 18, 2003: "No, we've had no evidence that Saddam Hussein was involved with September the 11th."[210] The President's need for evidence of an Al Qaeda-Saddam Hussein link may have precipitated the decision of the Bush-Cheney duumvirate to torture Al Qaeda detainees.

AMERICAN EMPIRE: BEFORE THE FALL

A companion fabrication was Saddam's alleged weapons of mass destruction. On August 26, 2002, Vice President Cheney exclaimed, "Many of us are convinced that Saddam will acquire nuclear weapons fairly soon…There is no doubt he is amassing [WMD] to use against our friends, against our allies, and against us." The Vice President also falsely informed then House Majority Leader Dick Armey that Saddam had miniaturized nuclear weapons, and that Al Qaeda had offered to act as human delivery vehicles, according to Barton Gelmon's *Angler*. On October 7, 2002, President Bush delivered a speech in Cincinnati to convince the public and Congress that he required authority to initiate war:

> The evidence indicates that Iraq is reconstituting its nuclear weapons program…Satellite photographs reveal that Iraq is rebuilding facilities at sites that have been part of his nuclear program in the past…he could have a nuclear weapon in less than a year…Facing clear evidence of peril, we cannot wait for the final proof, the smoking gun that could come in the form of a mushroom cloud.[211]

The speech pivoted on the CIA's 2002 National Intelligence Estimate. It projected a threat of Iraqi nuclear weapons within several months to a year only if it received sufficient fissile material from abroad. The President's State of the Union address on January 28, 2003, maintained: "The British Government has learned that Saddam Hussein recently sought significant quantities of uranium from Africa."[212] This statement was based on evidence that CIA Director George Tenet, the State Department's Bureau of Intelligence and Research, and other intelligence officials regarded as highly suspect.[213] President Bush also falsely asserted that Iraq possessed mobile biological weapons laboratories.

Saddam's interrogation after his capture confirmed that he had spe-ciously boasted of Iraq's WMD to deter an invasion from Iran, which he feared more than the United States.

Based substantially on White House deceit over WMD, Congress enacted the Authorization for the use of Military Force Against Iraq Resolution of 2002 by a vote of 296-133 in the House and 77-23 in the Senate. It unconstitutionally delegated to the President the decision to initiate war with Iraq.

But Iraq was no threat to the United States. No-fly zones since 1993 excluded Saddam from two-thirds of his own country. Kurds in the north enjoyed de facto independence. Numerous economic embargoes kept Iraq impoverished. Iraq was militarily and economically crippled in March 2003 when the United States invaded. Its WMD were optical illusions.

President Theodore Roosevelt was supremely jealous of President Abraham Lincoln because the latter achieved monumental fame largely from the Civil War. Roosevelt elaborated in 1910: "A man has to take ad-vantage of his opportunities, but his opportunities have to come. If there is not the war, you don't get the great general; if there is not the great occasion, you don't get the great statesman; if Lincoln had lived in times of peace, no one would know his name now."[214] The former President pre-dictably envied President Woodrow Wilson's opportunity to join in the mindless slaughters of World War I that Roosevelt had craved and urged.

Theodore Roosevelt epitomized the type of President the Founding Fathers intended to handcuff by entrusting the authority to initiate war ex-clusively to Congress. James Madison, father of the Constitution, prescient-ly elaborated "that the Executive is the branch of power most interested in war, and most prone to it." Madison added in his Helvidius letters that "war is in fact the true nurse of executive aggrandizement." Belligerency was:

> the parent of armies; from these proceed debts and
> taxes; and armies and debts and taxes are the known

instruments of the few. In war, too, the discretionary power of the Executive is extended; its influence in dealing out offices, honors, and emoluments is multiplied; and, all the means of seducing the minds, are added to those of subduing the force, of the people."[215]

Thomas Jefferson likewise applauded the separation of powers as an "effectual check on the dog of war."[216]

The Founding Fathers erected high institutional barriers to initiating war because they knew that the first casualty is the rule of law. Bush and Obama are conclusive proof.

Both have claimed unchecked power to kill any person anywhere in the world whom the president declares is collaborating with terrorism and is implicated in a continuing and imminent threat to United States persons.

Dana Priest reported in the *Washington Post*:

After the Sept. 11 attacks, Bush gave the CIA, and later the military, authority to kill U.S. citizens abroad if strong evidence existed that an American was involved in organizing or carrying out terrorist actions against the United States or U.S. interests, military and intelligence officials said. The evidence has to meet a certain, defined threshold. The person, for instance, has to pose "a continuing and imminent threat to U.S. persons and interests," said one former intelligence official. The Obama administration has adopted the same stance.[217]

President Obama, parroting President Bush, defines the "battlefield" as anywhere that an act of terrorism might conceivably be perpetrated. Accordingly, President Obama asserts unlimited power to order U.S.

citizens killed anywhere in the world with no judicial or legislative checks if he suspects they are implicated in international terrorism. King George III would be envious.

The National Security Agency flouted the Foreign Intelligence Surveillance Act of 1978 (FISA) from 2001-2007 by intercepting the emails and phone calls of American citizens on American soil on the President's say-so alone, without a judicial warrant. Congress then amended FISA in 2008 to authorize group warrants in violation of the Fourth Amendment, akin to a warrant to search every home in an entire State in the expectation that at least one criminal suspect might be discovered. A Central Intelligence Agency Inspector General report concluded that the illegal spying failed to thwart a single terrorist incident.

The FBI committed thousands of violations of the Patriot Act in obtaining business records without a warrant for non-terrorist investigations or without a proper written explanation of necessity. None of the violators have been punished or demoted.

Executive privilege or state secrets have been routinely invoked to frustrate congressional oversight, to operate secret government, and to protect government lawlessness from judicial scrutiny. White House assistants and secretaries are said to be constitutionally immune from congressional subpoenas. And presidential communications are withheld to block independent and fully informed congressional judgments about national security or monetary policy.

Crimes of torture in the name of national security are ignored.

Extraordinary rendition is employed to subject detainees to torture by foreign intelligence agencies outside the law.

Others have been held and interrogated in secret prisons abroad without legal or political accountability.

Italian authorities have convicted twenty-three CIA operatives in absentia for kidnapping Abu Omar in Milan for transport to Egypt where he was tortured. The United States refused extradite the accused CIA operatives.

Citizens and non-citizens are detained indefinitely as enemy combatants without accusation or charge based on "associate" status with Al Qaeda.

Military commissions that combine judge, jury, and prosecutor in a single branch, the very definition of tyranny according to the Founding Fathers, are employed for the trial of crimes that have been otherwise prosecuted without difficulty in civilian courts with all the trappings of due process.

Habeas corpus is unconstitutionally suspended by the Military Commissions Act of 2006.

Constitutionally protected speech short of incitement to violence is said to be a war crime.

Secretary of Treasury Henry Paulson cheerfully spent money without legal authority to assist failing financial institutions. The Federal Reserve Board conceals the identity of banks that received staggering sums to maintain solvency. It operates without serious congressional oversight.

United States Customs agents assert authority to inspect and to retain all information stored on laptops or cell phones without suspicion of wrongdoing.

The President negotiates Status of Forces Agreements governing the use of U.S. troops abroad unilaterally without statutory approval or treaty authorization.

The President refuses to enforce laws he has signed into being that he maintains are unconstitutional to circumvent the opportunity of Congress to override vetoes.

President Bush commutes the punishment of Vice President Cheney's Chief of Staff Scooter Libby for lying to the FBI about leaking the name of Valery Plame to discredit her husband for exposing lies about Iraq's alleged attempt to purchase uranium cake in Niger.

The rule of law applied to crimes perpetrated in the name of national security is absurdly derided as the earmark of banana republics.

George Orwell's *1984* has arrived in the United States, but a few decades late.

7

The American Empire's Bush-Cheney-Obama Triumvirate

President Obama confirms the American Empire as a fixture of the prevailing political culture, not a Bush-Cheney phenomenon. Obama has bought into the national security state featuring permanent war everywhere on the planet. The larger national motivation is to dominate the world for the excitement of domination. The narrower particular motivation of the President is to reduce coequal branches of government to vassalage, to place the President above the law, and to justify secret government without accountability. James Madison's admonitions about presidential wars have been vindicated.

Obama arrived at the White House with more knowledge of the Constitution and the philosophy of the Declaration of Independence than any other president in modern times. He was editor of the Harvard Law Review and a Professor of Constitutional Law at the University of Chicago Law School. He had served in the United States Senate. There, he had taken an oath to uphold and defend the Constitution of the United States. In comparison to Obama, President George W. Bush was a constitutional sub-literate.

Despite his intellectual acuity, Obama succumbed to the primal temptation of imperial power and domination. The wild enthusiasms that greeted his election to the White House by some champions of civil liberties were misplaced. As regards the psychology and practices of the American Empire, Obama and Bush are like Tweedle Dee and Tweedle Dum. The case of torture—a felony under the federal criminal code—is emblematic.

The current prohibition, enacted with both Republican and Democratic votes in Congress, is absolute, with no exceptions for ticking time bombs, Islamic radicals, or otherwise. Congress, however, is authorized to create exceptions by amending the statute. But it has not done so, and no President has ever asked for an exception.

President Bush and Vice President Cheney have boasted of authorizing waterboarding and other "enhanced interrogation techniques" against Al Qaeda suspects in the aftermath of 9/11. They tacitly concede they refrained from approaching Congress to seek an "Al Qaeda" exception for torture.

The United States prosecuted Japanese soldiers as war criminals for waterboarding American captives during World War II. Waterboarding creates an imminent fear of death that occasions prolonged mental trauma or distress, which falls within the definition of torture in the United States criminal code. (Waterboarding was employed by the CIA against Al Qaeda detainees on 283 occasions). The Bush-Cheney duumvirate predictably declined to prosecute officials implicated in waterboarding or other interrogation techniques tantamount to torture. The prosecutions would have implicated themselves. Bush's nonfeasance violated his unflagging constitutional obligation to take care that the laws be faithfully executed, not sabotaged or circumvented.

In 2003, Deputy Assistant Attorney General for the Office of Legal Counsel, John Yoo, advised that government officials could violate the criminal law with impunity in the name of fighting international terrorism: "If a government defendant were to harm an enemy combatant during an interrogation in a manner that might arguably violate a criminal prohibition (including murder), he would be doing so in order to prevent further attacks on the United States by the Al Qaeda terrorist network. In that case, we believe that he could argue that the executive branch's constitutional authority to protect the nation from attack justified his actions."[218]

After entering office, President Obama declared that waterboarding and sister "enhanced interrogation techniques" used by the Central Intelligence Agency against suspected Al Qaeda detainees constituted torture in violation of the Convention Against Torture and the criminal laws of the United States.[219] His Attorney General, Eric Holder, echoed that view under oath before the Senate Judiciary Committee. Like Bush, President Obama was saddled with a constitutional duty to faithfully execute the laws against torture or commit an impeachable high crime and misdemeanor. President Richard M. Nixon was impeached by the House Judiciary Committee for flouting his Article II obligation to faithfully execute the laws in the Watergate and related scandals.

But President Obama bettered Nixon's instruction and followed Bush's. He has refused even to investigate the Bush-Cheney torture crimes, which have been notoriously confessed. (The two have not asserted a "mistake of law" defense, i.e., that they relied in good faith on advice that waterboarding was legal). Obama has violated his oath of office because he covets unchecked presidential powers and wishes to project a political image of being "tough on terrorism."

Neither political ambitions nor optics justify flouting a constitutional duty. The President is crowned with the pardon power to excuse criminal wrongdoing for reasons of state. President Obama has shunned that constitutional prerogative for the crime of torture for fear of unleashing political wrath from the left wing of the Democratic Party. He remembers that President Gerald R. Ford's pardon of former President Richard M. Nixon cost him the 1976 presidential election with Jimmy Carter.

Obama's non-enforcement of the law against the former president and vice president, among others, has set a precedent endorsing flagrant White House lawlessness that will lie around like a loaded weapon ready for use by any President who claims a national security imperative.

Obama, Bush, and Cheney concur that the United States is engaged in a perpetual and global war against international terrorism. Obama has desisted from setting benchmarks that would signal the war's end. Like the Bush administration, he has championed the alarming and unprecedented legal notion that a nation can be at war with a tactic, which can neither sign a peace treaty nor be geographically circumscribed. According to Obama-Bush-Cheney, every square inch of the planet is a battlefield where military law or military force may be employed by the United States—whether in New Delhi, Karachi, Cairo, Tehran, New York City or otherwise. Civilian law is now subordinate to military justice.

No President of the American Empire, including Obama, will ever declare that the threat of international terrorism has fallen to below the threshold for war. The same is true for any Congress. Both branches fear that a future terrorist incident would expose them to criticism for alleged "softness" towards Al Qaeda. Contemporary politicians are either too unschooled or too timid to instruct the American people that accepting a measured risk of danger—including a second edition of 9/11—is necessary for freedom to breathe. The alternative is a police state in which everyone is detained because no one can swear under oath that he is incapable of evil, i.e. that he is a saint.

Permanent global warfare is irreconcilable with a Republic featuring checks and balances, transparency, and scrupulous protection of individual liberties. James Madison, father of the Constitution and chief architect of the Bill of Rights, admonished: "No nation could preserve its freedom in the midst of continual warfare."[220] Similarly, Alexander Hamilton, vocal proponent of a muscular presidency, nevertheless recognized in *Federalist No. 8* that war inexorably leads to the crippling of freedom:

> The violent destruction of life and property incident to war; the continual effort and alarm attendant on a state of continual danger will compel nations most attached to liberty, to resort for repose and security to

> institutions which have a tendency to destroy their civil
> and political rights. To be more safe, they at length be-
> come willing to run the risk of being less free. [221]

Like Bush, Obama claims unilateral authority to detain indefinitely United States citizens or non-citizens as national security threats, i.e. enemy combatants. The authority is said to rest on the Kafkaesque proposition that certain individuals are too dangerous to release but too innocent to prove guilty of an offense.

Then Senator Obama opposed enactment of the Military Commissions Act (MCA) of 2006. It empowered the President to detain citizens or non-citizens indefinitely without accusation or trial, and to prosecute non-citizens for alleged war crimes based on coerced testimony or torture before military commissions that combine judge, jury, and prosecutor.[222] But President Obama has accepted the sweeping powers conferred by the MCA, which are every bit as imperial as the powers of King George III assailed in the Declaration of Independence. Since his inauguration, he has not whispered a word urging repeal of the tyrannical legislation.

As a presidential candidate, Obama excoriated Bush's military commissions for flagrantly shortchanging due process. But as President, Obama has retained them as urgent for national security (albeit with minor procedural modifications). The claim of necessity is patently absurd. Commissions have been used but three times in more than eight years—involving David Hicks, Salim Hamdan, and Ali Hanza al Bahlul—to prosecute cases that are routinely tried in federal civilian courts. Australian David Hicks pled guilty to training in a terrorist training camp and received a nine-month prison sentence to be served in Australia. He neither killed nor threatened to kill any American. Salim Hamdan was tried and convicted of providing material assistance to a listed foreign terrorist organization and received a six-month prison term (he is now free in Yemen). He neither killed nor threatened to kill any American. The third detainee, Ali Hanza al Bahlul, was charged and convicted of conspiracy and producing a recruiting or motivational video for Al Qaeda. His case is on appeal. Al Bahlul never killed or threatened to kill any American. While military commissions have been largely dormant, the United States has secured approximately 200 international terrorist convictions in federal civilian courts.

Obama's unfulfilled pledge to close Guantanamo Bay is no material break from Bush-Cheney. Congress has barred that option by statute without incurring Obama's veto. More important, Obama has *not* pledged to either release Gitmo detainees or prosecute them for crimes in federal civilian courts with their panoply of constitutional protections against erroneous guilty verdicts.

He has announced plans to transfer enemy combatant detainees to a prison facility in Thompson, Illinois by 2011, barring Congressional opposition. But Guantanamo's constitutional evil is not geography. It is arbitrary indefinite detentions based on unproven, non-criminal, elusive associations with either Al Qaeda or a wholly or partially owned subsidiary or philosophical ally—a frightening executive power like King John's disappearing of adversaries into dungeons that provoked Magna Charta in 1215. As previously noted, the vast majority of Gitmo detainees who have filed habeas corpus petitions challenging the legality of their detentions have succeeded despite the government's authority to rely on classified evidence disclosed only to the judge. In one emblematic case, a detainee who had been tortured as an American spy for 18 months by Al Qaeda and Taliban was absurdly said to be an enemy combatant by the Obama Justice Department. Conservative United States District Judge Richard Leon voiced incredulity at the government's position, and declared the detention illegal.[223]

President Obama insists that he can circumvent the constitutional rights of Guantanamo Bay detainees to the Great Writ of habeas corpus in federal courts—recognized by the United States Supreme Court in *Boumediene v. Bush* (2008)--by transferring them to Bagram prison in Afghanistan. He was rebuffed by a United States District Judge, but has appealed the defeat.

Obama's continuing use of predator drone "targeted killings" or assassinations of Al Qaeda or Taliban suspects in Afghanistan and Pakistan, despite chronic civilian deaths viewed callously as "collateral damage," speaks further volumes about the American Empire. It respects no sovereignty but its own. International law is reduced to what the United States says it is. What would Obama do if Russia used predator drones to kill suspected Chechen terrorists hiding in the United States? He would retaliate with war!

According to published reports, the United States relies on intelligence gathered from Pakistani informants and video surveillance when targeting Al Qaeda adherents in Pakistani tribal areas for predator drone attacks.[224] But the reliability of the targeting has not been revealed. Nor has the process by which the executive branch vets the intelligence and chooses who is to be killed. Lawyers are said to assess whether each drone attack can be justified under international law. But their identities are unknown, as are the legal memoranda supporting the advice. Nor is it known whether the drone killings are audited to determine the accuracy of the intelligence. Recurring errors would mean that the United States is indiscriminately killing civilians, i.e. is committing war crimes with impunity. The probability of chronic intelligence mistakes seems high. With regard to detainees at Guantanamo Bay who were said by the government to be the "worst of the worst," the false positive error rate is astronomical—exceeding 80 percent.

A published column in *The New York Times,* authored by two experts, estimates the predator drone accuracy rate at 2%.[225] Congressional knowledge seems limited to cryptic information provided by the President to House and Senate Intelligence Committee leaders and the congressional leadership. Public information is confined to what has been leaked to the media.

The predator drone secrecy underscores the difference between the American Republic and the American Empire. In the latter, anything arguably relevant to national security trumps all other constitutional provisions. It is arguable, for example, that casting sunshine on predator drone targeted killings would cause the semi-friendly Pakistani government to fall and clue Al Qaeda as to its vulnerable points of penetration. Thus, transparency must yield to secrecy at the expense of crippling self-government. A Republic requires public or at least congressional knowledge of what the government is doing to enable citizens to register approval or disapproval or to support or oppose remedial or corrective legislation. Congress might rationally conclude that predator drone attacks are making more enemies than are being killed due to alarmingly deficient targeting. James Madison was explicit on the urgency of transparency to democracy:

> A popular Government, without popular information,
> or the means of acquiring it, is but a Prologue to a Farce
> or a Tragedy; or, perhaps both. Knowledge will forever
> govern ignorance: And a people who mean to be their
> own Governors, must arm themselves with the power
> which knowledge gives.[226]

At its inception, the American republic saluted transparency. The United States Senate ended its secret deliberations in 1794. President Washington resisted only one congressional request for information. The House of Representatives sought his negotiating gambits and instructions for negotiating the Jay Treaty with Great Britain. The President declined because the House had no legitimate constitutional role to play in treaty ratification. The Senate, entrusted with that responsibility, had been given and had scrutinized the information withheld from the House.

Leaks of classified information, such as the Pentagon Papers or the disclosure of the Terrorist Surveillance Program, have never caused national security injury. Former Secretary of Defense in the Nixon administration, Melvin Laird, refused to sign an affidavit in the *Pentagon Papers* litigation in the United States Supreme Court which would have asserted that diplomatic or national security harms would ensue from publication. The Secretary of Defense knew the worry was bogus. He proved correct. Prosecution of the Vietnam War was not handicapped when the Supreme Court in *New York Times v. United States* (1971) authorized publication of the 47-volume documentation of chronic presidential lies about the conflict.

Obama's embrace of the American Empire explains his about-face on disclosing photos of United States interrogation abuses in Freedom of Information Act litigation with the American Civil Liberties Union. As a presidential candidate, Obama had promised transparency in government. But on May 13, 2009, President Obama announced he would seek to block the release of as many as 2,000 photographs depicting abuses of detainees held by the United States abroad on the ground of national security. Obama elaborated:

> The publication of these photos would not add any additional benefit to our understanding of what was carried out in the past by a small number of individuals. In fact, the most direct consequence of releasing them, I believe, would be to further inflame anti-American opinion and to put our troops in danger.[227]

At Obama's request, Congress amended the Freedom of Information Act (FOIA) to exempt the photographs from release if Secretary of Defense Robert Gates certified that national security would be jeopardized, which he did.

A picture, however, is worth a thousand words. The photo of the young Vietnamese girl running naked down a street with her hair inflamed with napalm convinced more people to oppose the Vietnam War than all the teach-ins combined. Obama's statement that the photos depicting interrogation abuses would not add understanding to the ramifications of the wars in Iraq, Afghanistan, and against international terrorists everywhere was absurd. The My Lai massacre photographs of Vietnamese women and children slaughtered in a ditch enriched citizen understanding of the Vietnam War folly and augmented public pressure to prosecute the prime culprit, Lt. William Calley. The American people need to know or see what their government is doing when interrogating Al Qaeda suspects to determine whether they approve of or denounce the methods utilized and to urge adaptation of the law accordingly.

President Obama, like Bush, accepts the constitutionality of presidential wars initiated unilaterally without prior authorization from the legislative branch. He did not take issue with 2008 presidential candidate Hillary Clinton's assertion that as President she would be constitutionally empowered to obliterate Iran in retaliation against an Iranian nuclear attack on Israel.[228] Obama maintains that he is crowned by the Constitution to unilaterally initiate war against any country or any criminal group without a directive from Congress—a war making power exercised by King George III and specifically renounced by the Founding Fathers. Obama's Nobel Peace Prize address was crystal clear on that point: "I - like any head of state - reserve the right to act unilaterally if necessary to defend my nation."[229] Alexander Hamilton, however, explained in *Federalist 69*:

> The President is to be commander-in-chief of the army and navy of the United States. In this respect his authority would be nominally the same with that of the king of Great Britain, but in substance much inferior to it. It would amount to nothing more than the supreme command and direction of the military and naval forces, as first General and admiral of the Confederacy; while that of the British king extends to the declaring of war and to the raising and regulating of fleets and armies— all which, by the Constitution under consideration, would appertain to the legislature.[230]

THE AMERICAN EMPIRE'S BUSH

President Obama subscribes to the authority of Congress to empower the President alone to decide whether to initiate war, as was done regarding Iraq and Vietnam (with the Authorization for Use of Military Force Against Iraq Resolution of 2002 and the Gulf of Tonkin Resolution, respectively), despite the inarguable intent of the Constitution's makers to fasten that responsibility on Congress.

President Obama has accepted Bush-Cheney convictions that underwrite the American Empire's global military footprint. He agrees that international terrorists are sufficiently threatening to American sovereignty to cross the constitutional threshold for war. (No other nation in the world has characterized its conflict with international terrorism as "war" for purposes of the law.)

Accordingly, Obama maintains that terrorists must be attacked preemptively by the United States thousands of miles from American shores, not thwarted with defense forces at home in the unlikely event of an enemy attack. In his December 1, 2009 West Point presentation, he elaborated that, "To abandon [Afghanistan] now—and to rely only on efforts against Al Qaeda from a distance—would significantly hamper our ability to keep the pressure on Al Qaeda and create an unacceptable risk of additional attacks on our homeland and our allies."[231] But United States allies are not sending significant combat forces to Afghanistan because they know Al Qaeda is a non-existential threat without the staying power necessary to fight a war. Moreover, the doctrine of preemptive war is tantamount to war at the whim of the President. Then Congressman Abraham Lincoln elaborated in 1848:

> Allow the President to invade a neighboring nation, whenever he shall deem it necessary to repel an invasion, and you allow him to do so, whenever he may choose to say he deems it necessary for such purpose - and you allow him to make war at pleasure. Study to

see if you can fix any limit to his power in this respect, after having given him so much as you propose. If to-day, he should choose to say he thinks it necessary to invade Canada, to prevent Britain from invading us, how could you stop him? You may say to him, 'I see no probability of the British invading us,' but he will say to you, 'be silent; I see it, if you don't.'

Congressman Lincoln explained that the entire concept of preemptive war at the initiative of the President was unconstitutional and elevated the chief executive to a king:

The provision of the Constitution giving the war making power to Congress, was dictated, as I understand it, by the following reasons. Kings had always been involving and impoverishing their people in wars, pretending generally, if not always, that the good of the people was the object. This, our Constitution understood to be the most oppressive of all Kingly oppressions; and they resolved to so frame the Constitution that no one man should hold the power of bringing this oppression upon us. But your view destroys the whole matter, and places our President where kings have always stood. [232]

Obama echoes the fallacious myth so prominent in the *Truman Doctrine* that the United States has been saddled by God with a moral responsibility to dispatch troops abroad to prevent and to remedy human rights catastrophes like Darfur or Rwanda (although he has done nothing to fulfill that professed obligation). His West Point address amplified:

And we must make it clear to every man, woman, and child around the world who lives under the dark cloud of tyranny that America will speak out on behalf of human rights, and tend to the light of freedom and justice and opportunity and respect for the dignity of all peoples. That is who we are. That is the source, the moral source of America's authority...We will go forward with the confidence that right makes might, and with the commitment to forge...a world that is more secure....[233]

Obama's Nobel Peace Prize address was to the same effect:

More and more, we all confront difficult questions about how to prevent the slaughter of civilians by their own government, or to stop a civil war whose violence and suffering can engulf an entire region. I believe that force can be justified on humanitarian grounds, as it was in the Balkans, or in other places that have been scarred by war. Inaction tears at our conscience and can lead to more costly intervention later.[234]

If there were a moral imperative to employ military force abroad to prevent or to mitigate an ongoing genocide or comparable atrocities, then the United States would be obliged to invade China to rescue Tibetans and Uighurs, and to invade Russia to rescue Chechens. It would be compelled to invade the Democratic Republic of the Congo, Zimbabwe, and Iran to rescue their entire populations, to invade Burma to rescue the Karen and other ethnic tribes, to invade Sri Lanka to rescue Tamils, etc. But even the most ardent human rights champions like Nobel Prize winners Desmond Tutu or Jimmy Carter blanch at preaching such a sanguinary moral doctrine.

The public consensus is against any moral imperative to oppose by military force genocide or atrocities inflicted by a despotic government. Morality pivots on the probability of doing good as opposed to the probability of killing many and inviting endless wars. The most prudent course is to desist categorically from humanitarian military interventions for twofold reasons: they regularly fail or compound the misery of the populations to be helped, as in Somalia in 1992; and, there is no manageable definition that would prevent humanitarian interventions from leading to war at the whim of any would-be invader. Every country in the world can be censured for some human rights violations. Russia, for example, accused Georgia of genocide in South Ossetia, and dispatched military troops accordingly.

Obama also covets unbounded presidential power to blunt natural and inevitable economic downturns through staggering federal spending and budget deficits. He supported the Troubled Asset Relief Act of 2008. He pushed for an additional $800 billion stimulus spending extravaganza in 2009. He championed health care legislation in 2010 that will add hundreds of billions to the federal debt. He has presided over trillion dollar budget deficits, which he forecasts will persist for a decade. Bailout money was statutorily confined to financial institutions. But Obama showered money on two auto companies—Chrysler and General Motors—in the name of economic necessity. His legally dubious spending followed seamlessly from the prior administration. Bush's Secretary of Treasury, Henry Paulson, speaking of the takeover of Fannie Mae and Freddie Mac, as well as other megaseizures of failing Wall Street firms, boasted to a *Washington Post* reporter: "Even if you don't have the authorities—and frankly I didn't have the authorities for anything—if you take charge, people will follow."[235] If there are better ways to sneer at the rule of law by an executive branch officer sworn to uphold and defend the Constitution, they do not readily come to mind. Reporter Cho of the *Washington Post* continued in his report:

> Senior government officials said Paulson helped craft
> rescue programs for financial firms, though he was not
> sure he had an unquestionable legal basis for the initia-
> tives, including the bailouts of the failing investment
> bank Bear Stearns in March and the wounded insur-
> ance giant American International Group (AIG) in
> September. [236]

Every Empire seeks to shield its people from economic shocks or dis-
locations by government interventions in pursuit of a risk-free existence.
Think of the vast array of economic protections the British Empire offered the British East India Company, including protection from shipping
competition offered by American colonists. Obama has done the same
by pouring staggering sums on irresponsible financial institutions. Mad
economics, however, is routinely brilliant politics. Those whose jobs were
saved by Obama's profligacy will return the favor at the ballot box. But
the far larger number of unemployed whose plight stems from jobs that
never materialized because Obama's extravagance killed credit for start-
up companies are anonymous and politically invisible.

Presidents in the American Empire bow to its orthodoxies because
their preoccupation is day-to-day popularity and re-election. Obama is
no exception. He is no statesmanlike leader who breathes overarching
convictions about defending and enforcing the Constitution irrespective
of the immediate political fall-out. Only a person of uncommon intellectual courage will defy the American Empire's political culture and
disparage the primitive excitement of dominating other countries or people. Obama has failed that test of courage over Afghanistan and at every
other turn.

Expediency is Obama's North Star. He was against the state secrets
privilege to conceal constitutional wrongdoing, until he was in favor of it.
He was in favor of whistle-blower legislation covering intelligence agencies, until he was against it. He was against presidential power to hold

AMERICAN EMPIRE: BEFORE THE FALL

American citizens or residents as enemy combatants indefinitely without accusation of charge, until he was in favor of it. He was in favor of public financing of his presidential campaign, until he was against it. He was against the death penalty for the rape of children, until he was in favor of it. He was in favor of releasing photos of United States interrogation abuses, until he was against it. He was against individual Second Amendment rights to own handguns, until he was in favor of it. He was in favor of government transparency, until he was against it. He was against military commissions for the trial of war crimes, until he was in favor of it.

A President who wished to restore the American Republic would assail unchecked executive power in favor of a separation of powers and checks and balances. He would insist on the exclusive responsibility of Congress to decide whether to initiate war; acknowledge the sovereignty of "We the People" in lieu of an omnipotent executive branch; immediately withdraw all American troops from abroad and revoke all common defense treaties or executive agreements; treat international terrorists as criminal thugs, not as warriors or combatants; and inculcate in ordinary citizens a pride in self-government and a recognition that securing unalienable rights to life, liberty, and the pursuit of happiness for Americans is the sole mission of the United States.

Obama has done none of these things, not because they would undermine the safety, freedoms, or prosperity of the American people, but because he is a mental prisoner of the American Empire. He refuses to see the obvious. The United States would be *safer, freer, and wealthier* by reverting into the American Republic, which confined the military to protecting the United States, simpliciter.

With every American soldier tasked solely to protect Americans from immediate attack, re-introducing the draft might become politically viable. A draft would be healthy for two reasons. It would boost esprit de corps because the sole military objective would be the direct protection of American lives, not futile nation-building in Afghanistan, Yemen, Iraq, Pakistan, or otherwise. A draft would also restrain the President or Congress in the reckless use of military force in pursuit of utopian or Hail

Mary-type goals. In contrast, an all volunteer force encourages politicians to squander lives for trivial or hopeless causes because the volunteers come predominantly from the lower economic or social classes with inaudible political voices. The shelf life of the Vietnam War would have been much longer without the draft to spark sober second thoughts and analyses. The draft fueled the Fulbright hearings in the United States Senate beginning in 1966, which challenged the Pollyannaish war assumptions of President Johnson and his slavish Cabinet. In contrast, Congress has slept through every war post-dating the all-volunteer armed forces, including the Persian Gulf War, the Bosnian and Serbian wars, and the current wars in Iraq and Afghanistan and against international terrorism. The slumber has continued irrespective of the elusiveness of victory. In Afghanistan, Taliban and Al Qaeda have grown progressively stronger as the military presence of the United States and the International Security Assistance Forces have persisted for more than eight years—longer than all of World War II. The United States has suffered more than the equivalent of another 9/11 in American casualties in Iraq (approaching 5,000 deaths) without forging an Iraqi government that could survive an American military withdrawal. If draftees were serving in Iraq and Afghanistan, the public and congressional clamor for ending the wars there would be irresistible.

Withdrawing all troops from abroad would still leave the United States with eleven aircraft carriers and hundreds of submarines prowling throughout international waters, aircraft capable of reaching any country on earth, and spy satellites providing a constant world vigil. That projection is more than sufficient to identify and thwart imminent enemy attacks (as opposed to isolated criminal acts) on the United States, enabling crushing and instant retaliation if an attack were launched.

The United States should promise to leave all foreign countries undisturbed in their sovereignties and to remain neutral in wars between foreign countries. But it should equally threaten destruction worse than Hiroshima or Nagasaki to any country that attacks or begins an attack against the American people.

AMERICAN EMPIRE: BEFORE THE FALL

"Protect America Only" is what the Founding Fathers and the American Republic would champion. The strategy is not pacifist. It is not premised on a starry-eyed view of human nature or dangers from abroad. It disbelieves in the inclination of nations to follow the Bible, *Isaiah II* (King James Version): "They shall beat their swords into ploughshares, and their spears into pruning-hooks; nation shall not lift up sword against nation, neither shall they learn war any more." The strategy assumes the worst in human nature, and draws on thousands of years of treachery in international relations.

A "Protect America Only" national security strategy would eliminate the vast majority of the motivations for attacking the United States. There would be no resentments that fester in foreigners from the indignities of a United States military occupation, from interrogation or detention abuses targeting Muslims, from violations of national sovereignties, or from the killings of innocent civilian bystanders in pursuit of terrorist suspects.

There remains a risk of an ideological war against the United States initiated by a fanatical nation angered by America's democratic, secular, non-hierarchical credentials or fearful that the example of America's freedom and rule of law might awaken revolt among its own citizens or subjects. But no foreign nation has attacked the United States for that reason in more than 230 years. Even Al Qaeda, a non-state actor, seems to have perpetrated 9/11 (which posed no danger to United States sovereignty) because of America's global projection of its military and western culture in Saudi Arabia. The criminal acts of international terrorism were not provoked because of an ideological antipathy for freedom practiced in the United States. **Approximately one-half of the 9/11 hijackers were non-religious or impious**. In any event, upgraded intelligence, defenses, and border security combined with a devastating capacity for retaliation should deter even ideologically motivated war against the United States.

The "Protect America Only" strategy would be unthreatening to every foreign country and would not invite aggression. The United States would forswear the *initiation* of warfare against any other sovereign, just as Article 9 of the Japanese Constitution, dictated by then Supreme Commander for Allied Powers in Japan, General Douglas MacArthur, stipulates:

> Aspiring sincerely to an international peace based on justice and order, the Japanese people forever renounce war as a sovereign right of the nation and the threat or use of force as means of settling international disputes...In order to accomplish the aim of the preceding paragraph, land, sea, and air forces, as well as other war potential, will never be maintained. The right of belligerency of the state will not be recognized.[237]

As interpreted and applied, the article does not forbid self-defense forces to deter and to retaliate against foreign attacks. Indeed, the Japanese Self-Defense Forces (SDF) feature 240,000 active military personnel and the annual budget of the Japanese Defense Ministry approximates $50 billion.

Japan has not been threatened with attack in the 62 years since it adopted Article 9. Of course, the United States-Japanese Defense Treaty provides Japan with a United States nuclear umbrella and a commitment to come to its defense in case of war. No country, however, would be likely to attack Japan if the Defense Treaty ended because of Japan's formidable SDF.

The United States should offer peace to all countries irrespective of their democratic credentials. No society would risk annihilation while its own sovereignty remains unthreatened. The Soviet Union flinched in the 1962 Cuban Missile Crisis to avoid the risk of nuclear destruction when the United States was far less militarily dominant than it is today. And no nation has launched a military attack on the United States or its possessions since World War II, when the United States military was a shadow of its current profile.

8

A Reeducation For
Henry Kissinger

Former Secretary of State and National Security Adviser Henry Kissinger is widely accepted as gospel on national security matters because of his academic credentials and fabled government experience under Presidents Richard Nixon and Gerald Ford. He was also laurelled with a 1973 Nobel Peace Prize. But admiration for his putative sagacity is misplaced. He is a child of the American Empire, supporting all its orthodoxies and follies. His column published in *The Washington Post* on February 26, 2009, styled *"A Strategy for Afghanistan"* is definitive proof. An exhaustive analysis of the column follows because it demonstrates the sophomoric or incoherent reasoning of the American Empire by one of its most sophisticated and articulate exponents.

The title of the column itself is problematic. Kissinger never explains why the United States needs an Afghan *war* strategy. He shies from addressing the option of defending United States sovereignty and the American people from international terrorism with methods short of war: bolstering home defenses; upgrading intelligence collection and analysis; creating a crushing retaliatory capacity to deter potential attackers; and employing Special Forces to capture or kill Al Qaeda members. Kissinger simply accepts that the war in Afghanistan is a national security necessity as a matter of faith.

The United States had no Afghan policy whatsoever for most of its existence with no adverse effects. It provided modest and intermittent economic assistance to Afghanistan in the 1960s in its brainless competition with the Soviet Union for the sympathies or allegiance of every third world country. King Zahir Shah was overthrown in a bloodless coup in 1973 by a relative, Mohammed Daud Khan. He, in turn, was deposed by a Communist uprising in 1978. Neither event affected the safety, sovereignty, or wealth of the United States. It is highly probable that no living American can remember either date in Afghan history. Then came the ill-starred and ill-conceived Soviet invasion of 1979–a staggering blunder that marked the beginning of the end of the Soviet Empire. The invasion should have been greeted with glee by the United States instead of frenetic worry that the Soviet Union was poised to conquer all of South Asia and more as steps towards invading the United States itself.

The USSR would have been defeated in Afghanistan by Islamic insurgents even if the United States had provided no military or economic assistance whatsoever, including Stinger missiles, just as North Vietnam would have prevailed in the Vietnam War without Chinese or Soviet assistance. Charlie Wilson's War is not what destroyed the Red Army.

Afghanistan has never been an authentic country. Parochial Afghan loyalties have never yielded to national allegiances. Warlords dominate the countryside. Opium production and an illegal narcotics trade are rampant. Afghanistan's population is fractured among Tajiks, Hazaras, Pashtuns, Uzbecks, Turkmen, Nuristanis, Aimags, and Balochis. The rule of law, equality under the law, or the separation of religion from government (as in Ataturk's Turkey) has never taken hold. Corruption is ubiquitous, and extracts a steep financial toll on Afghan citizens. Dissent evokes frowns or repression. Sunni Islam is dominant. Its Afghan interpretation teaches female subjugation. They are denied education. They are compelled to wear chadors as punishment for uncontrollable male lust. They are stoned to death for adultery. Their legal rights are half that of men or less. The Afghan Parliament in 2009 passed a law, signed by President Hamid Karzai, which obligates wives to submit to the sexual demands of their husbands and to obtain spousal consent to travel outside the home.

Kissinger's counterfactual conviction that an American war in Afghanistan is a strategic imperative is on all fours with corresponding Afghan fallacies that foiled the British and Soviet Empires.

A landlocked nation with niggardly natural resources, Afghanistan has been a geostrategic inkblot for centuries. The twin British Afghan wars in the 1800s were fought to stave off a Russian invasion route to India— an artificial fear concocted by the British Empire to keep the populace alarmed. The only evidence of Russia's interest in challenging the British Raj was the Indian March of Emperor Paul (1801) and a Russo-French adventure that reached as far as the Aral Sea, roughly a thousand miles short of the Khyber Pass. It created a stir in London and touched off a war scare between Britain and Russia.

Every empire has its paranoia because it needs excuses for perpetual expansion, secrecy, and executive supremacy. The British Empire's paranoia was Russia. In 1904, the British invaded Tibet led by Sir Francis Younghusband. With Maxim guns and Enfield rifles, the soldiers killed thousands of Tibetans on their march from India. The Tibetans were coerced into a treaty that enabled Britain to post trade agents in Tibet. The British invasion rested on the delusion that Russia had a toehold there. The sealing off of Tibet by the Dalai Lama from the 13th century on had kept the British guessing and their imaginations fermenting. They concocted Tsarist plots, and resorted to great violence to pry open Tibet animated by their own fabrications.

The genuine motive for the 1839-1842 and 1878-1880 Afghan wars was to demonstrate to Great Britain's colonial possessions that challenges to its authority or pride through copycat insurrections would not be tolerated. Empires find even the slightest challenge to power intolerable. Great Britain was defeated handily in the First Afghan war. But its Empire was unaffected. (In the year of its defeat, Great Britain was victorious in its Opium War with China). Great Britain's mixed success in the Second Afghan war was equally irrelevant to its Empire.

The Soviet Empire invaded in 1979 for the sake of invasion, not for national security. Writing in *The Great Gamble: The Soviet War in Afghanistan*, Gregory Feiffer reports a Soviet staff officer's assertion that "no one ever actually ordered the invasion of Afghanistan." It came about from inertia and confusion under somnambulant Soviet leadership at the time. The precipitating factor was a desire to punish Afghanistan for its refusal to accept a Soviet puppet ruler and to behave as a Soviet vassal state. President Hazibullah Amin was killed, and replaced by Babrack Kamal.

Before the Soviet invasion, Afghanistan had never warred against Russia or the Soviet Union. It had no territorial designs on Soviet territory. It was not offering military bases to Soviet enemies. It held no significant economic resources. Its general celebration of Sunni Islam did not threaten to migrate into the atheist Soviet Union. A permanent Soviet occupation of Afghanistan would have been a permanent headache akin to Chechnya and a diversion of huge resources from opposing the United States.

The USSR, nevertheless, stupidly chose invasion with 40,000 military personnel. That number would ultimately climb to approximately 118,000 before the Soviet Union withdrew in humiliation nine years and 14,500 casualties later. The invading Red Army immediately encountered resistance. The most tenacious opponents were religious extremists—the mujahideen supported by Saudi Arabia, Pakistan, other Muslim nations, and the United States. The resistance leaders included future adversaries or enemies of the United States, for example, Osama bin Laden and Gulbuddin Hekmaytar. The resistance also included the seeds of the Taliban, which came to rule Afghanistan after the Soviet expulsion. Advanced United States weaponry such as stinger missiles that were supplied to expel the Red Army also ended up in the hands of Taliban or Al Qaeda forces. The Soviet experience in Afghanistan should have taught the futility of conquering its multiple tribes or ethnic groupings and establishing a strong and legitimate national government. United States assistance to the mujahideen, which flipped from ally to adversary, should have taught Kissinger the hazard of even provisionally supporting a nation or non-state actors who embrace a hostile political philosophy or ambitions. As Mark Twain observed, the difference between a man and a dog is that a dog will not bite the hand that feeds it.

Kissinger erroneously postulates that the ongoing war in Afghanistan is indispensable to preventing Taliban and Al Qaeda from regaining control there and launching a second edition of 9/11. But no evidence is marshaled to support the postulate. War against Taliban and Al Qaeda is creating new enemies because innocent civilians are invariably killed in pursuing and killing genuine terrorists through predator drones, high altitude bombings, or otherwise. Terrorists easily blend into the local population. Even America's Afghan puppet President Hamid Karzai, among other Afghan leaders, has vocally protested the civilian killings. Foreign military occupation also insults national pride and provokes resentments. These earmarks of the Afghan war *increase* rather than diminish the probability of a radical Islamic sequel to 9/11.

Kissinger ignores that the United States can best defend itself against potential mischief emanating from Afghanistan by withdrawing all troops there immediately and strengthening defenses against Al Qaeda in the United States. He ignores that Al Qaeda members like Osama bin Laden, who have already been indicted by federal grand juries for violating federal criminal prohibitions, can be captured or killed through covert operations utilizing methods similar to those that Israel employed to eliminate the Al Fatah assassins of eleven of Israel's Olympians at Munich in 1972. The Israeli Defense Force and Mossad collaborated in tracking down the known culprits. Michael Burleigh's *Blood and Rage* quotes a senior Mossad agent as follows: "If there was intelligence information, the target was reachable and if there was an opportunity we took it. As far as we were concerned we were creating a deterrence, forcing them to crawl into a defensive shell and not plan offensive attacks against us."[238] In seeking to cripple Al Qaeda, the United States does not confront a Hobson's choice of war or nothing, as Kissinger assumes.

Members of the executive branch would not be endowed with unchecked power to assassinate. Congress by statue could require a judicial warrant issued by a secret and based on probable cause to believe that the target had either killed or attempted to kill an American citizen and that capture was not feasible without undue danger to American captors. Records of these secret proceedings would be accessible to Congress and later to the public with an exception in the latter case for intelligence sources and methods whose disclosure would immediately and directly threaten lives.

Kissinger is unable to articulate a single coherent national security interest of the United States that rides on the outcome of the Afghan war. He sermonizes that if Taliban prevails, the fall-out will threaten Pakistan, India, Russia, China, and Indonesia—*but the United States is omitted from the list*: "The stakes [in the war] are high. Victory for Taliban in Afghanistan would give a tremendous shot in the arm to jihadism globally—threatening Pakistan with jihadist takeover and possibly intensifying terrorism in India, which has the world's third-largest Muslim population. Russia, China and Indonesia, which have also been targets of jihad Islam, could also be at risk." But Kissinger tacitly places the United States outside the Taliban danger zone.

His concocted fears about Taliban's danger to other nations are unconvincing. Pakistan displays far less eagerness or concern over defeating Taliban than does the United States. It is resisting cross-border troop attacks by the United States against Taliban or Al Qaeda forces within its territory. It balks at a large-scale military effort against Taliban in North Waziristan. It is unenthusiastic about Obama's Afghan "surge" featuring 30,000 additional U.S. soldiers. If a Taliban victory in Afghanistan actually threatened a jihadist takeover of Pakistan, it would be applauding the "surge" and inviting cross-border attacks. Similarly, if a Taliban victory in Afghanistan would signal danger to Russia, it would not have maneuvered (albeit ultimately unsuccessfully) to evict the United States from its Afghan air supply base at Manas, Kyrgyzstan, which would have handicapped the United States war effort. Kissinger's professed fretting over a

A REEDUCATION FOR HENRY KISSINGER

Taliban invasion of China to conduct jihad on behalf of 20 million Uighur Muslims in Xinjiang–a tiny fraction of the Chinese population—is laughable. China is daily extinguishing Uighurs and the Uighur culture through killings, torture, and an influx of Han Chinese. If either China or Pakistan truly felt threatened by Taliban, then they would be clamoring to offer their own combat troops to bolster the military efforts of the U.S. in Afghanistan. To this day, not a single soldier has been offered.

Kissinger maintains: "Heretofore, America has pursued traditional anti-insurgency tactics: to create a central government, help it extend its authority over the entire country and in the process bring about a modern bureaucratic and democratic society." But to believe such tactics might succeed in any circumstance is to believe in miracles or alchemy. Neither the United States nor any other country has been able to manufacture a democratic and stable nation out of whole cloth. The wise nation, like the wise man, knows what it doesn't know. At present, the human mind is not capable of understanding the endless complexities of nation-building well enough to make success in Afghanistan any more likely than a miracle. South Vietnam should have been a lesson for Kissinger. Despite stratospheric expenditures and hundreds of thousands of American troops, Kissinger was never able to establish a legitimate central government in South Vietnam. He was never able to extend the central government's control to the countryside dominated by the Viet Cong and North Vietnamese. He was never able to establish anything close to modern uncorrupt bureaucracies and a democratic dispensation. Kissinger offers no reasons to think Afghanistan is different from South Vietnam on this score.

Kissinger recognizes that utopian anti-insurgency tactics in Afghanistan will fail. He awkwardly and illogically elaborates: "The country is too large, the territory too forbidding, the ethnic composition too varied, the population too heavily armed. No foreign conqueror has every succeeded in occupying Afghanistan. Even attempts to establish centralized Afghan control have rarely succeeded and then not for long. Afghans seem to define their country in terms of a common dedication to independence but not to unitary or centralized government."

But Kissinger fails to draw the obvious conclusion from the hopelessness of manufacturing a centralized Afghan government, i.e., that United States troops should immediately withdraw. He inexplicably supports another utopian military strategy to win the hearts and minds of the Afghan population, and then sputters into conclusory blather or non-sequiturs for achieving that objective:

> The truism that war is, in effect, a battle for the hearts and minds of the Afghan population is valid enough in concept. The low standard of living of much of the population has been exacerbated by 30 years of civil war. The economy is on the verge of sustaining itself through the sale of narcotics. There is no significant democratic tradition. Reform is a moral necessity. But the time scale for reform is out of sync with the requirements of anti-guerilla warfare. Reform will require decades; it should occur as a result of, and even side by side with, the attainment of security—but it cannot be a precondition for it.

If war is about winning the hearts and minds, why does Kissinger place reform in the caboose rather than in the locomotive of the victory train? That placement guarantees defeat. It is commonplace that guerillas can be defeated only if opposed by the general population that shares real time intelligence with the government or occupying power and denies insurgents safe houses. But popular support can only be conferred upon a government that is reasonably uncorrupt, honors the rule of law, and sports efficient and effective police and national defense forces. President Karzai's government is notoriously corrupt. His re-election was marred by massive fraud. The rule of law is a joke. The production of opium is climbing. Neither the police nor the Afghan National Army protects the citizenry from Taliban or Al Qaeda. Civilian deaths are chronic. Government services like education, hospitals, or roads are acutely deficient. President Karzai's bodyguards are American, not Afghan.

Kissinger is clueless about raising the standard of living in Afghanistan. He has no plan for ending economic reliance on opium or drug trafficking. He has no plan for inculcating democratic customs. He has no plan for implementing reforms or even describing what they would be. He has no plan for attaining security for the general population. He is like the admiral in World War II who insisted that Nazi submarines could be thwarted by boiling the ocean.

Kissinger continues: "The military effort will inevitably unfold at a pace different from the country's political evolution. Immediately, however, we are able to make sure that our aid efforts, now diffuse and inefficient, are coherent and relevant to popular needs. And much greater emphasis should be given to local and regional entities."

But as Kissinger previously recognized, military force, without the hearts and minds of the people, is futile. It is cruel, heartless, and purposeless to send Americans to die for an unpopular foreign government. That is precisely what Kissinger and his predecessors did in Vietnam. The United States military effort galloped leagues ahead of the political legitimacy of the South Vietnamese regime. As a consequence, tens of thousands of United States soldiers died for nothing, and South Vietnam was conquered by North Vietnam because the GOSV lacked popular support.

Kissinger's recommendation to make current economic or humanitarian aid "coherent and relevant to popular needs" in lieu of inefficiency and incoherence is juvenile. No government makes inefficiency or incoherence official policy. These flaws emerge from institutional incentives and political dynamics. In addition, Kissinger never identifies the demarcation line between relevant and irrelevant popular needs. Are Gallop Polls to be administered to identify popular needs? Are local referenda to be organized? Are loya jirgas, or "grand assemblies" to be summoned? Kissinger is also silent about how to make government bureaucracies coherent and relevant to their mission. He served several years as Secretary of State presiding over a large bureaucracy. Yet his Memoirs do not sub-stantiate that the State Department was earmarked by bureaucratic co-herence. Kissinger's insinuation that he knows how to streamline and perfect bureaucracies is reminiscent of Glendower's boast to Hotspur in Shakespeare's *Henry IV, Part I,* that he can summon spirits from the vasty deep: Glendower: "*I can call spirits from the vasty deep!*" Hotspur: "*Why so can I; or so can any man. But will they come when you do call for them?*"[239]

Kissinger's exhortation to place greater emphasis on local and re-gional entities is misplaced, like recommending devolution for the tot-tering Holy Roman Empire. At present, the Afghan central government is clinging to power by the skin of its teeth. President Karzai is disparagingly styled the "Mayor of Kabul." Afghanistan is splintered into countless tribal or ethnic power centers or enclaves. If more resources are diverted to local or regional officials, the central government will become a façade propped up by the United States military. And local and regional entities have shown themselves ill-suited to defeating Taliban or Al Qaeda. They routinely turn to collaboration in exchange for safety or money.

Kissinger advises: "Military strategy should concentrate on pre-venting the emergence of a coherent, contiguous state within the state controlled by jihadists." That is as useless as declaring: "Military strategy should concentrate on preventing Taliban and Al Qaeda from overthrow-ing the Government of Afghanistan and on making the Afghan National Army invincible."

Kissinger fatuously observes: "Gen. David Petraeus has argued that, reinforced by the number of American forces he has recommended, he should be able to control the 10 percent of Afghan territory where, in his words, 80 percent of the military threat originates. This is the region where the 'clear, hold and build' strategy that had success in Iraq is par-ticularly applicable."

History has proven, however, that generals are vastly too optimistic. Take Vietnam as an example. There, more troops were always said as guaran-teed to bring victory within grasp. On November 21, 1967, General William Westmoreland delivered a major speech at the National Press Club in which he announced that the United States would soon be running victory laps in Vietnam. The headline in the *Washington Post* read, "WAR'S END IN VIEW-WESTMORELAND," reminiscent of President Bush's "Mission accomplished" pronouncement about Iraq. But the light at the end of the tunnel never came. Further, United States control of territory is futile if–as with Afghanistan—the government lacks strength and popular legitimacy. All the United States military equipment and support that was given to the Shah of Iran was impotent to save him from the Iranian Revolution. Even if General Petraeus were correct, his strategy would reduce the immediate violence but would do nothing to create an Afghan government capable of standing on its own. United States troops would be trapped forever in Afghanistan to prevent Taliban or Al Qaeda from becoming dominant. General Petraeus himself recognizes that there is no military victory in Iraq, only a political solution. He testified to that effect before Congress antecedent to the Iraqi surge. The General continues to maintain that for the surge to have lasting impact, the Iraqi government must find national political legitimacy.

In addition, the "clear, hold, and build" strategy in Iraq is far from a proven success because it does not address the fragility of Iraq's political dispensation. Whether the Iraqi government would survive intact if United States troops are completely withdrawn is problematic. If simply killing the enemy and controlling territory were substantially sufficient to win wars, then the United States would have prevailed many times in Vietnam. The North Vietnamese and Vietcong were decimated in the Tet Offensive of 1968. According to United States figures, 4,959 Vietcong were killed and 1,862 captured while 232 American and 300 South Vietnamese troops died with 929 and 747, respectively, being wounded. Yet Tet was a military success for North Vietnam in convincing the United States it could not win.

The Strategic Hamlet Program in Vietnam (a clear, hold, and build strategy) proved a spectacular failure. Its fatal flaws, however, do not prevent Kissinger from recommending a carbon copy in Afghanistan, which is doomed to fail for the same reasons it stumbled in South Vietnam. The following excerpts from *The Pentagon Papers* explain:

The Strategic Hamlet Program was much broader than the construction of strategic hamlets per se. It envisioned sequential phases which, beginning with clearing the insurgents from an area and protecting the rural populace, progressed through the establishment of GVN infrastructure and thence to the provision of services which would lead the peasants to identify with their government. The strategic hamlet program was, in short, an attempt to translate the newly articulated theory of counter-insurgency into operational reality. The objective was political though the means to its realization were a mixture of military, social, psychological, economic and political measures.[240]

The problem with the apparent consensus that emerged early in 1962 was that the principal participants viewed it with different perspectives and expectations. On the U.S. side, military advisors had a set of preferences that affected their approach to the Strategic Hamlet Program. They wanted to make RVNAF more mobile, more aggressive, and better organized to take the offensive against the Viet Cong. They were, consequently, extremely leery of proposals that might lead it to be tied down in strategic defenses ("holding" after "clearing" had been completed) or diverted too much to military civic action undertakings.

The American political leadership, insofar as a generalization may be attempted, can be said to have been most concerned with the later phases of the program—those in which GVN services were provided, local governments established, and the economy bolstered. Military clearing operations were, to them, a distasteful, expensive, but necessary precondition to the really critical and important phases of the effort.

Both of these U.S. groups had perspectives different from those of the Diem administration. In the U.S. view, the insurgents were only one of Diem's enemies; he himself was the other. Therefore, America felt that the process of pacification could proceed successfully only if Diem reformed his own government. It was precisely to achieve these goals simultaneously that the U.S. agreed to enter a "limited partnership" with GVN in the counter-insurgent effort. The Strategic Hamlet Program became the operational symbol of this effort.

President Diem—unsurprisingly—had a very different view. His need, as he saw it, was to get the U.S. committed to South Vietnam (and to his administration) without surrendering his independence. He knew that his nation would fall without U.S. support; he feared that his government would fall if he either appeared to toady to U.S. wishes or allowed any single group too much power—particularly coercive power. The Strategic Hamlet Program offered a vehicle by which he could direct the counter-insurgent effort as he thought it should be directed and without giving up either his prerogatives to the U.S. or his mantle to his restless generals.

The Strategic Hamlet Program predictably collapsed.

In his 2009 column in the Washington Post, Kissinger blathers: "In the rest of the country, our military strategy should be more fluid, aimed at forestalling the emergence of terrorist strong points." But any military strategy severed from wining the loyalty and enthusiasm of the indigenous population is doomed. Kissinger has no ideas about how to accomplish that feat, and recommends strengthening local military chieftains who will enervate the national government and demoralize the Afghan National Army: "[Our military strategy] should be based on close cooperation with local chiefs and coordination with their militias to be trained by U.S. forces—the kind of strategy that proved so successful in Anbar province, the Sunni stronghold in Iraq." But the fragmentation of Afghan insurgents in defeating the Soviet Union was precisely what occasioned Taliban's rise to power in 1996. Afghan local chiefs have never been loyal to Kabul. Moreover, the jury is still out on whether U.S. training of Sunni local militias in Anbar independent of the Shiite dominated government in Baghdad will prove farsighted or folly.

Kissinger pontificates that his Afghan strategy "is a plausible approach, though it seems improbable that the 17,000 reinforcements President

Obama recently committed is enough." The strategy is implausible, however, because it is empty of a concrete political dimension. Kissinger also betrays a scandalous indifference to the horrors of war. United States General William Tecumseh Sherman maintained that war is hell. But Kissinger is callously willing to sacrifice the lives and limbs of American soldiers based on a strategy that at best is "plausible," which means "seemingly or apparently valid." He sets a higher standard for appraising Obama's plans than he does his own. He disparages the 17,000 troop increase in Afghanistan as being an "improbable" (or not likely) success story, which still satisfies the threshold for plausibility. Further, Kissinger is silent as to why 17,000 additional troops would be too few. No President with a sense of decency would commit more troops than necessary for a mission because it would mean more senseless American deaths.

Kissinger solemnly preaches: "In the end, the fundamental issue is not so much how the war will be conducted but how it will be ended." But the former is dispositive of the latter. In Vietnam, the strategy and tactics of the United States in conducting the war dictated the final outcome— complete victory for North Vietnam. If the Afghanistan war is conducted with indigenous political fragmentation, popular disgust with government fraud, corruption, nepotism, ineptitude, and a reliance on local warlords, the end will be the Taliban or Al Qaeda celebrating in Kabul.

Kissinger declares: "Afghanistan is almost the archetypal international problem requiring a multinational solution for a political framework to emerge." But if that is true, the United States should not dispatch a single soldier to Afghanistan until all the international players Kissinger has in mind have agreed to be part of the solution. Further, Kissinger is unable to identify a single successful multinational solution to any national problem during the last century, including Darfur, Somalia, Bosnia, Kosovo, or the Democratic Republic of the Congo. And his solution is as absurd as believing that nations can be cajoled into beating swords into plowshares and making war obsolete.

This is Kissinger's multinational fantasy: "In Afghanistan, [a multinational solution] is achievable only if its principal neighbors agree on a policy of restraint and opposition to terrorism. Their recent conduct argues against such prospects. Yet history should teach them that unilateral efforts at dominance are likely to fail in the face of countervailing intervention by other outside actors." Kissinger ignores that history teaches that nations do not learn from history. The United States caper in Vietnam championed by Kissinger persisted despite knowing that North Vietnam would prevail in part because of substantial outside intervention by the Soviet Union and Communist China. It would be utterly reckless–like the Charge of the Light Brigade—for the United States to dispatch soldiers to die based on a strategy that presumes Russia, India, Pakistan, Iran, and China will all desist from pursuing their short term interests in Afghanistan to the benefit of the United States.

Russia is no ally. It quarrels with the United States over South Ossetia and Abkhazia in Georgia, membership of Ukraine in NATO, strategic arms, human rights, and anti-missile systems in Poland, the Czech Republic, and Romania. Russia remembers the massive United States assistance to the mujahideen in Afghanistan to repel the 1979 Soviet invasion. It is naturally inclined to return the favor. But Russia must temper its desire for revenge. To support Taliban or Al Qaeda would be to risk a spread of radical Islam to Chechnya, Dagestan, and Ingushetia. On the other hand, the risk to Russia of a radical Islamic blow-back is tiny compared to the massive damage Russia could inflict on the United States by offering Taliban and Al Qaeda weapons and money to kill the growing number of United States military forces there. (Iran has promised Russia to oppose Islamic radicalism within its sphere of influence in exchange for Russian softness on Iran's nuclear program). Russia has every incentive to make the United States post-9/11 invasion of Afghanistan a second United States Vietnam.

India's paramount foreign policy nemesis is Pakistan, with which it has warred three times since independence in 1947. India covets close relations with Afghanistan to put Pakistan in a vice. The 2009 Mumbai international terrorist incident corroborated that India's interest is in opposing Taliban and Al Qaeda in both Afghanistan and Pakistan. Of all

Afghanistan's neighbors, India's interests are most congruent with those of the United States there.

Pakistan's territorial claims against Afghanistan—it has never been reconciled to the British "Durand line"—make it at least a semi-champion of constant Afghan convulsions encouraged by Taliban or Al Qaeda attacks. That would facilitate a predominant Pakistani influence in Afghanistan, possible Islamic recruits to conduct a jihad against India over Kashmir, and a weakened Afghan ability to defend its own sovereignty or borders. Pakistan craves a decrepit Afghanistan that it can dominate, the opposite objective of the United States. And it fights India's growing prominence there through economic assistance or otherwise. Pakistan is implicated in a recent bombing of the Indian Embassy in Kabul. On the other hand, Pakistan's government is also fearful of radical Islam practiced by Taliban or Al Qaeda, which could provoke the overthrow of Pakistan's semi-secularism. Thus, the amount of aid and comfort Pakistan extends to the two terrorist groups is grudging. Pakistan's government is ambivalent about the United States daily violations of Pakistan's sovereignty with remotely piloted predator drones that indiscriminately kill terrorists and innocent civilians. It applauds the killings of its radical Islam enemies, but simultaneously, like Pakistani citizens, feels humiliated by the need to rely on Western help. Overall, a stable Afghanistan with President Karzai in power would be a Pakistani setback.

China's interest in Afghanistan is largely to support its ally Pakistan, and to keep the United States bogged down in an unwinnable war. An endless Afghan war means less United States military resources devoted to Taiwan, South Korea, or Japan, and lesser rebukes over the Chinese religious and ethnic persecutions of Tibetans and Uighurs. China would receive little or no benefit from a resolution of Afghanistan that would extricate the United States and cripple Taliban or Al Qaeda. At best, Afghanistan or Pakistan might cease as places where the Uighur diaspora might train to fight the People's Liberation Army. China successfully lobbied the United States and the United Nations to have the East Turkestan Islamic Movement listed as a terrorist organization. China's optimal outcome in Afghanistan would be a nation semi-convulsed enough to require a continuing United States war machine, but not sufficiently fragile to risk a takeover by Taliban or Al Qaeda.

Iran is the arch-enemy of the United States. The two clash over nuclear weapons, the Holocaust, Israel, Hezbollah, Hamas, state sponsorship of terrorism, Iranian support for the Iraqi resistance, and a United States apology for its 1953 overthrow of Prime Minister Mohammed Mossaddeq in favor of a reviled Shah. Iran would relish making Afghanistan a United States quagmire. That does not require unsparing Iranian support for Taliban or Al Qaeda. All that is necessary is for Iran to keep Afghanistan in upheaval by insuring that none of the competing tribes or factions prevails. Iran would deplore Taliban or Al Qaeda ascendancy because both radical Sunni groups are anathema to Iran's Shiites. Further, the Hazara, a Persian speaking Shiite population in central Afghanistan, would be persecuted by Taliban or Al Qaeda. Thus, Iran's objective in Afghanistan for the foreseeable future is permanent war with no victors.

Kissinger's happy convergence of interests and actions between Afghanistan's neighbors, Afghanistan, and the United States is an *ignus fatuus*. Any President who relied on its validity to deploy American soldiers would be guilty of negligent homicide or worse.

Kissinger's fantasy continues:

> To explore such a vision, the United States should propose a working group of Afghanistan's neighbors, India, and permanent members of the U.N. Security Council. Such a group should be charged with assisting in the reconstruction and reform of Afghanistan and establishing principles for the country's international status and obligations to oppose terrorist activities. Over time, America's unilateral military efforts can merge with the diplomatic efforts of this group. As the strategy envisioned by Petraeus succeeds, the prospects

for a political solution along these lines would grow correspondingly.

Kissinger's proposed working group would consist of Pakistan, India, Tajikistan, Turkmenistan, Uzbekistan, China, Russia, the United States, Great Britain, and France. Many have clashing interests in the reconstruction and reform of Afghanistan. Russia, China, Tajikistan, Turkmenistan, and Uzbekistan, for instance, have no desire to assist the transformation of Afghanistan into a vibrant, secular democracy. The quintet is non-democratic. It fears a democratic example on its doorstep. Some of the quintet is non-secular. None is a United States ally that would cheer a United States success story in Afghanistan. The working group is a non-starter.

Kissinger recognizes the improbability of his working group nostrum. It has no chance of success without the goodwill, altruism, or high statesmanship of Russia and Pakistan: "The precondition of such a policy is cooperation with Russia and Pakistan. With respect to Russia, it requires a clear definition of priorities, especially a choice between partnership or adversarial conduct insofar as it depends on us."

Kissinger is mute on why Russia might believe its national interests advanced by cooperating to relieve the United States of its Afghan albatross and enabling a redirection of United States military resources toward Russia. The price of the Afghan war being paid by the United States is staggering: deaths of U.S. soldiers; hundreds of billions in wasted defense expenditures; and the creation of new enemies through the ineluctable killings of innocent Afghan civilians, humiliations of the indigenous population, and detention abuses. Kissinger falsely insinuates that the United States confronts a binary choice in its relationship with Russia: either partner or adversary. But the two are not mutually exclusive. The United States and Russia might find common ground over the reduction of strategic arms or international terrorism, yet be adversaries over Iran's nuclear ambitions, the United States presence in Iraq, South Ossetia or Abkhazia, or anti-missile systems in Poland, the Czech Republic, or

Romania. Insofar as the United States might offer Russia concessions in non-Afghanistan matters in exchange for Afghan cooperation, Kissinger is silent as to what linkage might be appropriate.

As for Pakistan, Kissinger is unable to articulate any reason for confidence that greater military collaboration over Afghanistan would be forthcoming. Yet Pakistan is a lynchpin to his strategic Afghan vision: "The conduct of Pakistan will be crucial. Pakistan's leaders must face the fact that continued toleration of the sanctuaries - or continued impotence with respect to them - will draw their country ever deeper into an international maelstrom." But the latter observation is false. President Pervez Musharraf tolerated Taliban and Al Qaeda, yet was toppled by internal political forces angered by his militaristic despotism. His overthrow left Pakistan's dilemma in dealing with radical Islam unchanged. The incumbent, President Ali Zadari, has taken more aggressive military action against Taliban and Al Qaeda strongholds. But his precarious hold on power stems from indigenous opposition, not an international maelstrom.

Kissinger's stumbles continue:

> If the jihadists were to prevail in Afghanistan, Pakistan would surely be the next target - as is observable by activity already taking place along the existing borders and in the Swat Valley close to Islamabad. If that were to happen, the affected countries would need to consult each other about the implications of the nuclear arsenal of Pakistan being engulfed or even threatened by jihadists. Like every country engaged in Afghanistan, Pakistan has to make decisions that will affect its international position for decades.

But a Taliban or Al Qaeda victory in Afghanistan would not necessarily lead the jihadists to turn against Pakistan. Indeed, Pakistan supported

Taliban during its Afghan rule prior to 9/11. Jihadists did not generally attack Pakistan when it turned more secular after the death of President Zia al Haq.

To be sure, jihadists covet theocracy. A jihadist assassinated Benazir Bhutto during her 2008 Pakistani presidential campaign. Jihadists attempted assassinations of President Musharraf. They have imposed Sharia law in Pakistan enclaves near the border with Afghanistan. A jihadist victory in Afghanistan, however, would diminish their threat to Pakistan. After acquiring power, Iran's mullahs turned to making money and perfecting the art of corruption rather than carrying their revolution elsewhere. When Taliban ruled Afghanistan in the years before 9/11, it had no eyes on invading Pakistan.

But suppose jihadists did attack Pakistan. Kissinger declares that the affected countries would need to consult each other over what to do with Pakistan's nuclear arsenal. But he never defines the phrase "affected countries." Since nuclear weapons are implicated and their use could trigger a nuclear winter or nuclear retaliation, every nation in the world could be affected by putting Pakistan's nuclear arsenal in the hands of jihadists. How would they all consult one another? Would India consult China over how to respond? Would the United States consult Saudi Arabia? Further, Pakistan's nuclear arsenal is already threatened by jihadists. They sought to topple President Musharraf and are equally antagonistic towards President Ali Zardari. The Mumbai terrorist attacks and assault on Sri Lanka's cricket players in Pakistan similarly showed the strength of jihadists.

Contrary to Kissinger, countries currently engaged in Afghanistan do not need to make decisions that will affect their international positions for decades. Suppose the United States declined to extend official recognition to a new Taliban government in Afghanistan. How could that estrangement affect the United States international standing there thirty years later? Kissinger vastly inflates the importance of Afghanistan to defeating terrorism and jihadists worldwide to create an artificial sense of foreboding or crisis to transfix public attention on his jejune and misconceived op-ed.

A REEDUCATION FOR HENRY KISSINGER

Kissinger returns to exaggeration in asserting: "Other countries, especially our NATO allies, face comparable choices." But the Baltic States of Estonia, Latvia, and Lithuania do not worry about Afghanistan. Neither do scores of other nations. Taliban ruled Afghanistan from 1996-2001. The overwhelming majority of nations were unaffected. Why would things change if Talban reasserted control? Kissinger sermonizes:

> But save for some notable exceptions, public support for military operations is negligible in almost all NATO countries. It is possible, of course, that Obama's popularity in Europe can modify these attitudes - but probably only to a limited extent. The president would have to decide how far he will carry the inevitable differences and face the reality that disagreements concern fundamental questions of NATO's future and reach. Improved communications would ease this process. It is likely to turn out, however, that the differences are not procedural. We may then conclude that an enhanced NATO contribution to Afghanistan's reconstruction is more useful than a marginal military effort constrained by caveats. But if NATO turns into an alliance a la carte in this manner, a precedent that can cut both ways would be set. Those who tempt a U.S. withdrawal by their indifference or irresolution evade the prospect that it would be the prelude to a long series of accelerating and escalating crises.

NATO was formed in 1949, however, to oppose the Soviet Union at the height of the Cold War. The USSR featured a well-trained Red Army, atomic weapons, top-flight scientists, and an industrial base capable of supporting a sustained war. NATO's geographic preoccupation was Europe. Kissinger, however, never asks why NATO should extend its sphere into Afghanistan. Taliban or Al Qaeda is not the Red Army. Not a single NATO country is worried about losing their sovereignty to either terrorist organization. (In contrast, some are fearful of Russia on that score). Why should NATO send a single soldier to fight in Afghanistan? And why should the United States care if NATO disintegrated? It does not depend on any NATO member to defend its sovereignty.

Kissinger tacitly dismisses public opinion in NATO countries opposed to military engagement in Afghanistan as unschooled. But on matters of war and peace, popular opinion has regularly proven more prescient than the convictions of Kissinger-like experts. The public was ahead of politicians and pundits in the United States in recognizing that the Vietnam War was unwinnable and that the domino theory was a scarecrow. Ditto for recognizing that Iraq and Afghanistan are unwinnable wars if the objective is the creation of stable, secular, legitimate, and democratic countries.

Kissinger's Gotterdammerung fear of NATO disunity over Afghanistan brings new meaning to the operatic in foreign policy. Afghanistan is a cipher on NATO's national security map. NATO is no more likely to fracture over troops there than it is to rupture over whether to offer NATO membership to Georgia or Ukraine.

Kissinger gallops to a meaningless conclusion: "President Obama said on Tuesday night that he 'will not allow terrorists to plot against the American people from safe havens halfway around the world.' Whatever strategy his team selects needs to be pursued with determination. It is not possible to hedge against failure by half-hearted execution." Kissinger accepts President Obama's pronouncement without questioning its wisdom or accuracy. If Obama means what he said, then Iran, Pakistan, Yemen, Somalia, Indonesia, North Korea, Syria, Lebanon, and Palestine must logically join Afghanistan on the roster of nations to be invaded by the United States because all house terrorists plotting against America. Further, why should the United States be frightened into military action by nefarious plots thousands of miles away when such plots can be thwarted before Americans are harmed by defensive measures at home and deterred by the threat of Hiroshima-like retaliation? Consider how the United States addresses threats from missiles. Anti-missile defenses are constructed and retaliation is promised. The United States does not destroy missiles before launch that could reach the United States in countries such as Russia, China, or North Korea. The United States responded to the Cuban Missile Crisis of 1962 with a naval quarantine, not with a blitzkrieg invasion and incineration of Cuba.

Kissinger's column demonstrates the mental inventiveness necessary to justify the American Empire's permanent global war.

9

Restoring
The American Republic

Individuals or corporate interests will deny truths that threaten their jobs or profits or expose the triviality or pointlessness of their professions. A company that builds military transport aircraft for use in Afghanistan or Iraq will dispute that both conflicts are wars of choice, not necessity.

A university professor or government official whose training and career depend on American initiatives to democratize the world by force, threats, or economic carrots and sticks will button his ears to the idea that the objective is constitutionally illicit and unachievable. The countless businesses and employees who profit financially from the war against international terrorism by selling counter-terrorism products or services will never accept the truth that the terrorist danger falls short of the threshold for war. Nor will they acknowledge that the terrorism threat can and should be defeated by an aggressive enforcement of the criminal law in federal civilian courts, coupled with Special Forces to eliminate terrorists who cannot be captured and brought to justice.

Government officials routinely leave for more profitable ventures in the private sector and acquire an economic interest in magnifying the terrorism danger to keep government contracts flowing or expanding.

AMERICAN EMPIRE: BEFORE THE FALL

The American Empire's countless economic parasites will resist a restoration of the American Republic. An equally large number will balk to maintain their self-esteem derived from thinking they are saving the nation from jihadists.

The American Republic, in contrast, preached the superiority of a more perfect union that secures the blessings of liberty only for Americans in lieu of a global, swaggering American Empire seeking control and influence by military force or economic enticements. That idea will seem novel to contemporary Americans, and novel ideas are inherently upsetting to human nature.

Galileo confronted resistance from power centers in promoting the heliocentric theory of the universe to replace its time-honored geocentric rival. To believe Galileo meant disbelieving the inerrancy of the Bible and papal encyclicals—which were pillars of both Church and secular power in the 1600s. Thus, the astronomer's theories and those of Copernicus were listed in the Pope's Index of Forbidden Books. Five centuries elapsed before Galileo was semi-exonerated by Pope John Paul II.

For seventy years, the American Empire's orthodoxies have indoctrinated citizens and leaders alike in the belief that the United States has been obligated by divine Providence to make the world safe for democracy and freedom, and to crush every conceivable foreign danger before it germinates. The indoctrination has succeeded substantially because citizens of the American Empire derive psychic excitement or fulfillment from controlling others by force of arms. The same psychological dynamic sustained the British Empire and explained why its global military projection remained constant and popular whether guided by Prime Minister Benjamin Disraeli, an overt imperialist, or William Gladstone, a professed opponent of Empire. Political culture and orthodoxies are vastly more important than personalities in predicting a nation's national security policies. Obama's emulation of Bush is no surprise O Henry ending to the 2008 election campaign.

From time immemorial, western culture, with no exception for Great Britain or the United States, has honored domination for the sake of domination. Its electrifying heroes that transfix mass audiences are epitomized by Achilles, Hector, Alexander the Great or Lancelot, not by Nestor, Socrates, or Aristotle. Conquest or brute strength is admired more than reason, wisdom, humility, or self-restraint. An Empire is the ultimate trophy of power, but is akin to a Superbowl triumph in its moral emptiness. For that reason, the American Empire's exponents will blind themselves to the debased reality of what they have wrought.

Stalin's show trials of his Bolshevik comrades in 1930s are instructive on that score. The Soviet dictator accused major Communist Party figures of espionage, treason, or economic sabotage. The alleged crimes were transparent concoctions. But the stalwart Communist defendants accepted their respective grisly fates with resignation because they could not accept that their revolutionary and bloodstained exertions had given birth to a Mephistopheles. Zinvoviev, Kamenev, Bukharin, Tomsky, and Rykov pled guilty.

Similarly, the countless government officials and private businessmen that have devoted their careers to building and expanding the American Empire will find it psychologically traumatic to disown their handiwork as adolescent, unconstitutional, or immoral.

Convincing the American people and political leaders to restore the American Republic and to honor the Charter Documents will confront strong economic, political, psychological, and moral headwinds. But the same could have been said of the anti-slavery movement in the United States at its inception.

Where responsibility lies for restoring the Republic is clear.

In Shakespeare's *Julius Caesar*, Cassius scolds Brutus for acquiescing in Caesar's burgeoning power and submitting to vassalage:

"Why, man, he doth bestride the narrow world
Like a Colossus, and we petty men
Walk under his huge legs and peep about
To find ourselves dishonourable graves.

AMERICAN EMPIRE: BEFORE THE FALL

> Men at some time are masters of their fates:
> The fault, dear Brutus, is not in our stars,
> But in ourselves, that we are underlings."[241]

That idea of personal responsibility for the course of history similarly found expression in Edward R. Murrow's analysis of the ascendancy of McCarthyism during his March 9, 1954 CBS television show *See It Now:*

> We cannot defend freedom abroad by deserting it at home. The actions of the junior senator from Wisconsin have caused alarm and dismay amongst our allies abroad and given considerable comfort to our enemies and whose fault is that? Not really his. He didn't create the situation of fear; he merely exploited it, and rather successfully. Cassius was right: "The fault, dear Brutus, is not in our stars, but in ourselves." [242]

As Ralph Waldo Emerson wrote, "There is properly no history; only biography."[243]

Contrary to President Harry Truman, the buck in the United States does not stop in the Oval Office. It stops with every citizen, whose voice and vote directs the nation's destiny. The American Republic foists responsibility for morally agonizing decisions of war and peace; due process; the separation of church and state; abortion; the death penalty; rights of racial, ethnic, religious, or other minorities; economic liberty versus corporate or social welfare; etc. onto the shoulders of every citizen. They cannot be shirked by blaming the President, Vice President, Congress, the Supreme Court, or Platonic Guardians. The life of a vassal or serf is not worth living. That is why the Declaration of Independence fastens a *duty* on every subjugated subject or citizen to seek the overthrow of their oppressors.

RESTORING THE AMERICAN REPUBLIC

The American Republic will be restored from its metamorphosis into Empire only if the people either demand or support restoration. A demand could emerge from spontaneous popular sentiments dissatisfied with the results of Empire. But the ordinary citizen lacks the wisdom and boldness to discern the Empire's moral or political decadence or the genius of the American Republic. The vast majority is invariably imprisoned by prevailing orthodoxies.

That leaves new political leadership as the instrument for restoration by inspiring the American people to embrace the thrill, excitement, and challenges of self-government, personal responsibility, and defending the Constitution in both letter and spirit. The nation's Charter Documents provide the blueprint for a new birth of the American Republic. Collectively, they recommend enactment of an omnibus statute to protect and defend the Constitution of the United States, "The Constitution Act of 2010."

The President should be exposed to criminal prosecution or impeachment for initiating war without an express statutory directive, or for intentionally deceiving Congress or the American people about a material fact for the purpose of obtaining authorization to initiate war.

War against non-state actors, such as Al Qaeda or Taliban, or tactics, like terrorism, should be prohibited. In particular, Congress should expressly renounce the current war against international terrorism and direct the President to treat international terrorists as criminals.

No monies of the United States should be expended to support military bases or troops abroad except in times of war expressly declared by Congress.

No monies of the United States should be expended to execute any defense treaty commitment of the United States, including NATO, the Japanese Defense Treaty, and the South Korean Defense Treaty.

No monies of the United States should be expended to support a United States mission at the United Nations.

No monies of the United States should be expended to gather or analyze foreign intelligence that is not shared with the House and Senate

Intelligence Committees and Members of Congress who take a secrecy oath.

The Foreign Intelligence Surveillance Act should be amended to require individualized warrants issued by the Foreign Intelligence Surveillance Court in lieu of group warrants, and to impose reasonable time limits on retaining information on American citizens.

The President should be prohibited from classifying any information except pursuant to a specific statute detailing the classification criteria. No classified information should be withheld from Congress. Executive privilege to conceal information from Congress based on a claimed generalized presidential need for confidentiality should be prohibited. Any executive branch official who refuses to answer questions under oath before a congressional committee or to appear before a congressional committee by invoking executive privilege should be fined $100,000 for each day of contempt or non-responsiveness to Congress.

The state secrets privilege should be abolished by Congress. As in criminal cases under the Classified Information Procedures Act of 1980, the government in civil cases should be required to choose between disclosing state secrets indispensable to a fair trial or accepting a default judgment or particular adverse findings of fact.

The President should be prohibited from detaining persons as enemy combatants without accusation or trial.

Military commissions should be abolished.

Extraordinary renditions should be prohibited.

No individual or organization should be designated as terrorist based on secret evidence.

No monies of the United States should be expended to execute a law to which the President appended a signing statement.

No monies of the United States should be available to invest in private enterprise.

The Federal Reserve Board should be abolished.

The President should be prohibited from regulating greenhouse gas emissions by delegation from Congress.

National security letters, i.e., administrative subpoenas with no judicial authorization, should be abolished.

The President should be prohibited from unilateral negotiation of executive agreements relating to national security.

The National Security Advisor and White House Counsel should be subject to Senate confirmation.

Deficit spending should be prohibited absent two-thirds majorities in the House and Senate, and federal taxes should be capped at 10 percent of national income.

The American people should insist that every candidate for the House, Senate, or President support each of these legislative ideas to restore the American Republic and the Constitution as understood by the Founding Fathers.

It would mark the finest hour of the United States.

If the American people do nothing, the American Empire will end in their ruination.

NOTES

CHAPTER 1

1. Joseph Alois Schumpter, The Economics and Sociology of Capitalism, ed. Richard Swedberg (Princeton, Princeton University Press, 1991), 142-143.

No one calls its imperialism when a state, no matter how brutally and vigorously, pursues concrete interests of its own; and when it can be expected to abandon its aggressive attitude as soon as it has attained what it was after. The word "imperialism" has been abused as a slogan to the point where it threatens to lose all meaning, but up to this point our definition is quite in keeping with common usage, even in the press. For whenever the word "imperialism" is used, there is always the implication—whether sincere or not—of an aggressiveness, the true reasons for which do not lie in the aims which are temporarily being pursued; of an aggressiveness that is only kindled anew by each success; of an aggressiveness for its own sake, as reflected in such terms as "hegemony," "world dominion," and so forth. And history, in truth, shows us nations and classes—most nations furnish an example at some time or other—that seek expansion for the sake of expanding, war for the sake of fighting, victory for the sake of winning, dominion for the sake of ruling. This determination cannot be explained by any of the pretexts that bring it into action, by any of the aims for which it seems to be struggling at the time. It confronts us, independent of all concrete purpose or occasion, as an enduring disposition, seizing upon one opportunity as eagerly as the next. It shines through all the arguments put forward on behalf of present aims. It values conquest not so much on account of the immediate advantages—advantages that more often than not are more than dubious, or that are heedlessly cast away with the same frequency—as because it is conquest, success, action. Here the theory of concrete interest in our sense fails. What needs to be explained is how the will to victory itself came into being.

Expansion for its own sake always requires, among other things, concrete objects if it is to reach the action stage and maintain itself, but this does not constitute its meaning. Such expansion is in a sense its own "object," and the truth is that it has no adequate object beyond itself. Let us therefore, in the absence of a better term, call it "objectless." It follows for that very reason that, just as such expansion cannot be explained by concrete interest, so too it is never satisfied by the fulfillment of a concrete interest, as would be the case if fulfillment were the motive, and the struggle for it merely a necessary evil—a counterargument, in fact. Hence the tendency of such expansion to transcend all bounds and tangible limits, to the point of utter exhaustion. This, then, is our definition: imperialism is the objectless disposition on the part of a state to unlimited forcible expansion.

…Our analysis of the historical evidence has shown, first, the unquestionable fact that "objectless" tendencies toward forcible expansion, without definite, utilitarian limits—that is, nonrational and irrational, purely instinctual inclinations toward war and conquest—play a very large role in the history of mankind. It may sound paradoxical, but numberless wars—perhaps the majority of all wars—have been waged without adequate "reason"—not so much from the moral viewpoint as from that of reasoned and reasonable interest. The most herculean efforts of the nations, in other words, have faded into empty air. Our analysis, in the second place, provides an explanation for this drive to action, this will to war—a theory by no means exhausted by mere references to an "urge" or an "instinct." The explanation lies, instead, in the vital needs of situations that molded peoples and

classes into warriors—if they wanted to avoid extinction—and in the fact that psychological dispositions and social structure acquired in the dim past in such situations, once firmly established, tend to maintain themselves and to continue in effect long after they have lost their meaning and their life-preserving function. Our analysis, in the third place, has shown the existence of subsidiary factors that facilitate the survival of such dispositions and structures—factors that may be divided into two groups. The orientation toward war is mainly fostered by the domestic interests of ruling classes, but also by the influence of all those who stand to gain individually from a war policy, whether economically or socially.

2. *See* page 112.

3. See Office of Professional Responsibility, *Report*, "Investigation into the Office of Legal Counsel's Memoranda Concerning Issues Relating to the Central Intelligence Agency's Use of "Enhanced Interrogation Techniques" on Suspected Terrorists," July 29, 2009, 63-64.

During the Office of Professional Responsibility (OPR)'s investigation into the Office of Legal Counsel's memoranda concerning issues relating to the Central Intelligence Agency's use of "enhanced interrogation techniques" on suspected terrorists, an OPR investigator asked John Yoo, who wrote the infamous "Torture Memos," to explain how the torture statute would interfere with the President's war making abilities. The following is their exchange:

OPR investigator:	*I guess the question I'm raising is, does this particular law really affect the President's war-making abilities...*
John Yoo:	*Yes, certainly.*
OPR investigator:	*What is your authority for that?*
John Yoo:	*Because this is an option that the President might use in war.*

OPR investigator:	*What about ordering a village of resistants to be massacred?...Is that a power that the President could legally —*
John Yoo:	*Yeah. Although, let me say this. So, certainly that would fall within the Commander-in-Chief's power over tactical decisions.*
OPR investigator:	*To order a village of civilians to be [exterminated]?*
John Yoo:	*Sure.*

4. See page 125.

5. Barak Obama, "Nobel Peace Prize Acceptance Speech," Oslo, Norway, December 10, 2009.

6. Steven Erlanger, "Yemen Says It's Arrested 3 Qaeda Militants," *New York Times*, January 7, 2010.

7. Catherine Herridge, "Senators Urge Administration to Transfer Alleged Bomber to Military Custody," *FoxNews.com*, http://www.foxnews.com/politics/2010/01/25/senators-urge-administration-transfer-christmas-bomber-military-custody/, (accessed on April 16, 2010).

8. Associated Press, "Somali Man Charged in Attack on Danish Cartoonist," *USA Today*, January 1, 2010.

9. Ibid.

10. Scott Shane, "A Year of Terror Plots, Through a Second Prism," *New York Times*, January 13, 2010.

11. General Douglas McArthur — May 15, 1951

12. H. L. Mencken, *In Defense of Women*, (Alfred A. Knopf, 1922), 38.

13. Thomas Jefferson, "First Inaugural Address." Keynote address, Senate Chambers, Washington D.C., 4 March 1801.

14. Grover Cleveland, "First Inaugural Speech." Washington D.C., March 4, 1885.

15. David N. Balmforth., *America's Coming Crisis: Prophetic Warnings, Divine Destiny*, Utah, USA: Horizon Pub & Dist Inc, 1998, 14.

NOTES

16. Victor Davis Hanson, "Iraq: Hard Hearts," *Hoover Digest: Research and Opinion on Public Policy,* Summer Vol. 3, 2007.

17. Moscow has maintained a fleet in Sevastopol for more than two centuries in the Tsarist, communist and post-Soviet eras. But, with less than a decade to run on its lease, Russia is worried that its days there are numbered. It has launched what appears to be a campaign to reabsorb Sevastopol into its own borders, sparking a full-blown diplomatic dispute that appears to be a flashpoint in a new cold war. For Russia, it is a question of reversing what it considers to be a grave historical injustice. Russian empress Catherine the Great purloined Sevastopol for Russia in the 18th century. But, in 1954, then Soviet leader Nikita Khrushchev transferred ownership of the Crimea from the Russian Soviet Socialist Republic to the Ukrainian Soviet Socialist Republic, apparently on a whim. But when the USSR disintegrated, Russia discovered one of its naval jewels and a region it considered its own in a foreign country. With Ukraine's pro-Western leadership pushing to join NATO, Russia's bitterness has turned to open hostility. Military clashes between Russia and Ukraine are highly probable within the foreseeable future.

18. Barack Obama, "Remarks by the President in Address to the Nation on the Way Forward in Afghanistan and Pakistan." United States Military Academy at West Point, West Point, New York, December 1, 2009.

19. Patrick E. Tyler, "U.S. Strategy Plan Calls for Insuring No Rivals Develop a One Superpower World." *New York Times,* March 8, 1992.

20. Project for the New American Century, 1997, "Statement of Principles," http://www.newamericancentury.org/statemen-tofprinciples.htm, (accessed on February 4, 2010).

21. Thomas Donnelly, "Rebuilding America's Defense: Strategy, Forces and Resources for a New Center," *The Project for a New American Century,* 2000.

22. William Pitt, "Of Gods and Mortals and Empire," *Truthout,* 2003, http://www.nogw.com/download/_07_gods_mortals_empire.pdf, (accessed on February 22, 2010).

23. Paul Wolfowitz, "Briefing to the Pentagon," Arlington, Virginia, September 13, 2001.

24. George W. Bush, "Remarks by the President at the 2002 Graduation Exercise of the United States Military Academy," United States Military Academy, West Point, New York, June 1, 2002.

25. Robert Barnes, "McCain to Georgian President: 'Today We Are All Georgians,'" *The Washington Post,* August 12, 2009.

26. John F. Kennedy, "Berlin Speech," Rudolph Wilde Platz, Berlin, June 26, 1963.

27. James Madison, Speech, <u>Constitutional Convention</u> (<u>1787-06-29</u>), from Max Farrand's *Records of the Federal Convention of 1787,* vol. I (1911), p. 465

28. Linda J. Bilmes, "The Three Trillion Dollar War: The True Cost of the Iraq Conflict," *LA Times,* July 2, 2009, http://articles.latimes.com/2009/jul/02/opinion/oe-bilmes2?pg=2.

29. Abraham Lincoln, "Address Delivered at the Dedication of the Cemetery at Gettysburg." In *Great Speeches,* (New York: Dover Publications, 1991) 103.

30. Lewis Carroll, In *Alice's Adventures in Wonderland*, (London: Penguin Books, 1998).

31. Associated Press, "Obama: No rights for Bagram prisoners," *MSNBC,* February 20, 2009, http://www.msnbc.msn.com/id/29308012/, (accessed on April 16, 2010).

32. Shakespeare, William, *The Oxford Shakespeare: Julius Caesar,* (Oxford World's Classics: the Oxford Shakespeare), New York: Oxford University Press, USA, 2008.

33. Letter Addressed to the Inhabitants of the Province of Quebec, Oct. 26, 1774, Journal of the Continental Congress 1, 108 (W. Ford ed. 10904).

34. Adam Liptak. "Obama About-Face Goes to High Court." *New York Times*, September 15, 2009, New York edition.

35. Marvin Myers, "The Jacksonian Persuasion," *American Quarterly* 5, no. Spring, 1953, 14.

NOTES

36. Alexander Hamilton, John Jay, and James Madison *The Federalist Papers* (London: Penguin Classics, 1987).

37. Ibid.

38. Richard Armey, "AUTHORIZATION FOR USE OF MILITARY FORCE AGAINST IRAQ RESOLUTION OF 2002", *C-Span*, October 10th, 2002,http://www.c-spanvideo.org/congress/?q=node/77531&appid=596118772 (accessed April 15, 2010).

39. John Bonifaz, *Warrior-king: the case for impeaching George W. Bush* (New York: Nation Books, 2003) 15.

40. John Bonifaz, *Warrior-king: the case for impeaching George W. Bush,* (New York: Nation Books, 2003), 16.

41. Gene Healy, "A Presidency Worth Celebrating," February 18, 2008. http://www.cato.org/pub_display.php?pub_id=9230, (accessed February 22, 2010).

42. Jeffrey H. Morrison, *The Political Philosophy of George Washington,* (Baltimore, John Hopkins University Press) 56, 143.

43. Louis Fisher, "Domestic Commander in Chief: Early Checks By Other Branches," *Cardozo Law Review* 29, no.3 (Fall 2008), 981-982, http://loc.gov/law/help/usconlaw/pdf/cardozo_fisher.pdf (accessed on April 16, 2010)

44. Louis Fisher, "Domestic Commander in Chief: Early Checks By Other Branches," *Cardozo Law Review* 29, no.3 (Fall 2008), 982, http://loc.gov/law/help/usconlaw/pdf/cardozo_fisher.pdf, (accessed on April 16, 2010).

45. Martti Juhani Rudanko, *James Madison and Freedom of Speech: Major Debates in the Early Republic,* (Lanham, University Press of America, 2004), 64.

46. Ibid.

47. David Cole, "Enemy Aliens," *Stanford Law Review* 54 No.5, no. May (2002), 953.

48. Victor W. Sidel and Barry S. Levy, "War, Terrorism, and Public Health Symposium Article - Part I: Global Challenges to Public Health," *The Journal of Law, Medicine, and Ethics* 31 (2003), 521.

49. Justice Jackson, *West Virginia State Board of Education Et Al. v. Barnette Et Al.,* Supreme Court of the United States, 319 U.S. 624, June 14, 1943, http://www.law.umkc.edu/faculty/projects/ftrials/conlaw/barnette.html (accessed April 12, 2010)

50. Thomas Paine, *Common Sense,* (London: Createspace, 2009).

51. Alexander, Matthew, "I'm Still Tortured by What I Saw in Iraq" *The Washington Post*, November 30, 2008, sec. Outlook.

52. John M. Broder, "Climate Change Seen as Threat to U.S. Security," *New York Times (New York City)*, August 9, 2009, New York edition.

53. Todd Pitman, "Africans Wary on New US Command for Continent." *USA Today (North America)*, September 30, 2008.

54. Editorials, "Tough on Israel," *Washington Post,* July 30, 2009, http://www.washingtonpost.com/wp-dyn/content/article/2009/07/29/AR2009072903167.html (accessed on April 16, 2010).

55. John D. McKinnon, "Cheney Visits Georgia, Slams Russian Actions," *The Wall Street Journal*, http://online.wsj.com/article/SB122051771846298917.html, (accessed on February 22, 2010).

56. Jose Donoso, *A House in the Country*, 1st Aventura ed. (New York: Vintage, 1985).

57. Edward Burke, *Reflections on the Revolution in France,* ed. Leslie George Mitchell, (New York, Oxford University Press June 15, 2009), 289.

CHAPTER 2

58. Henry Wadsworth Longfellow. *The Landlord's Tale: The Midnight Ride of Paul Revere. In The Poetical Works of H. W. Longfellow: Complete.* (London: Dicks, 1868), 181-182.

59. Reference to the quote: " For as in absolute governments the king is law, so in free countries the law ought to be king," Thomas

Paine, *Common Sense,* (New York: Peter Eckler Publishing Co, 1918), 36.

60. Ralph Waldo Emerson, "Concord Hymn," 1836, *The Complete Works of Ralph Waldo Emerson: Poems* (Boston: Houghton Mifflin Company, 1918), 158.

61. U.S. Constitution. Preamble.

62. James Madison, *The Federalist 51: The Structure of the Government must Furnish the Proper Checks and Balances Between the Different Departments.* In *The Federalist Papers,* (London: Penguin Books, 1987) 318.

63. Adam Smith, *An Inquiry into the Nature and Causes of the Wealth of Nations,* In *Essays on Philosophical Subjects,* (London: T. Cadell and W. Davies, 1795), 81.

64. Alexander Hamilton, *The Federalist Papers,* ed. Ian Shapiro (New Haven, Yale University Press, 2009), 19.

65. John Jay, *The Federalist No. 4: Concerning Dangers from Foreign Force and Influence.* In *The Federalist Papers.(* London: Penguin Books, 1987), 97.

66. John Quincy Adams, *Address on US Foreign Policy*, 1821.

67. Edmund Burke, *Remarks on the Policies of Allies with Respect to France*, In *Reflections on the Revolution in France.* (London: Penguin Books, 1968), 65.

68. James Madison, *Memorial and Remonstrance Against Religious Assessments.* In *The Writings of James Madison: 1783-1787* (London: GP Putnam's Sons, 1901), 183.

69. C.J. Chivers, "Pinned Down, A Sprint to escape Taliban Zone," *New York Times,* (2009), http://www.nytimes.com/2009/04/20/world/asia/20ambush.html?pagewanted=1&_r=2, (accessed on April 22, 2010).

70. Greg Jaffe, "U.S. retreat from Afghan valley marks recognition of blunder," *The Washington Post*, Thursday, April 15th, 2010, http://www.washingtonpost.com/wp-dyn/content/article/2010/04/14/AR2010041401012.html, (accessed on April 15th, 2010).

71. Alissa J. Rubin, "U.S. Forces Close Post in Afghan 'Valley of Death'", *New York Times,* April 14, 2010, http://www.nytimes.com/2010/04/15/world/asia/15outpost.html?partner=rss&emc=rss, (accessed on April 15, 2010).

72. Greg Jaffe, "U.S. retreat from Afghan valley marks recognition of blunder," *The Washington Post*, April 15th, 2010, http://www.washingtonpost.com/wp-dyn/content/article/2010/04/14/AR2010041401012.html, (accessed on April 15th, 2010).

73. Lolita C. Baldor, *"Obama Advisor Downplays Threat of Al Qaeda Haven,"The Washington Times,* (2009), http://www.washingtontimes.com/news/2009/oct/04/adviser-afghan-government-must-do-better/?page=2

74. Associated Press, "More in U.S. are getting away with murder," *MSNBC,* December 8, 2008, http://www.msnbc.msn.com/id/28116857/ (accessed on April 17, 2010)

75. Letter to the Editor, "A Life of Worth, Overlooked," *Washington Post,* July 5, 2009, http://www.washingtonpost.com/wp-dyn/content/article/2009/07/04/AR2009070402024.html (accessed on April 17, 2010)

76. John Kerry, *Vietnam Veterans against the War Statement*, April 22, 1971, http://www2.iath.virginia.edu/sixties/HTML_docs/Resources/Primary/Manifestos/VVAW_KerrySenate.html, (accessed on April 22, 2010).

77. Alissa J. Rubin, "U.S. Forces Close Post in Afghan 'Valley of Death'", *New York Times,* April 14, 2010, http://www.nytimes.com/2010/04/15/world/asia/15outpost.html?partner=rss&emc=rss, (accessed on April 15, 2010).

78. Ibid.

79. Ibid.

80. John Henry Clippinger, *A Crowd of One: The Future of Individual Liberty*, Perseus Books Group 2001, pg. 129

NOTES

CHAPTER 3

81. George Washington. *Farewell Address to the People of the United States.* September, 1796, (Washington: Government Printing Office, 1862), 10.

82. Ibid.

83. Ibid, 11.

84. John Quincy Adams. July 4th Address, Washington, D.C. 1821.

85. In Latin " Inter arma silent leges." Marcus Tullius Cicero. *Pro Milone.* 52 B.C.

86. *The Alien Act,* July 6, 1798; Fifth Congress; Enrolled Acts and Resolutions; General Records of the United States Government; Record Group 11; National Archives.

87. Bill Ong Hing, *Defining America Through Immigration Policy,* (Philidelphia: Temple University Press, 2004), 18.

88. Ibid.

89. Ibid.

90. Edwin Williams, *The Book of the Constitution: Containing the Constitution of the United States*, (New York: Henry Mason, 1833) 58.

91. Alexander Hamilton, John Jay, and James Madison, *The Federalist Papers* (University of Virginia, 1788), Section 10, Electronic Text Center, http://etext.lib.virginia.edu/toc/modeng/public/HMJFedr.html, (accessed on January 29, 2010).

92. Edwin Williams, *The Book of the Constitution: Containing the Constitution of the United States*, (New York: Henry Mason, 1833) 58.

93. "John & Abigail Adams: The Alien and Sedition Acts," *PBS*, August 26, 2005, http://www.pbs.org/wgbh/amex/adams/peopleevents/e_alien.html, (accessed on April 22, 2010).

94. James Madison, Letter to Thomas Jefferson, April 2, 1797.

95. James Madison, in *Abridgement of the Debates of Congress, From 1789 to 1856,* (New York: D. Appleton and Company, 1857), 554.

96. A punitive expedition in the Northwest Territory on November 4, 1790, also known as St. Clair's Defeat, the "Columbia Massacre," or the "Battle of the Wabash". This was the greatest defeat of the American army by Native Americans in history with some 623 American soldiers killed about 50 Native Americans.

97. James Monroe, *State of the Union Address,* December 2, 1823, *In State of the Union Addresses,* (Kessinger Publishing, LLC, 2004), 64.

98. United States Senate, "1801-1850, January 16, 1837, Senate Reverses a Presidential Censure," http://www.senate.gov/artandhistory/history/minute/Senate_Reverses_A_Presidential_Censure.htm (accessed on April 14th, 2010)

CHAPTER 4

99. Alexis de Tocqueville, *Democracy in America, Volume 1*, (New York: The Colonial Press, 1900), 201.

100. *In* Chales K. Burdick, *The Law of the American Constitution: Its Origin and Development*, (New York: G.P. Putnam's Son's, 1922), 3.

101. Charles Francis Adams, ed., *The Works of John Adams, Second President of the United States, Vol. 6*, (Boston: Chales C. Little and James Brown, 1851)(220)).

102. *The Jeffersonian Cyclopedia: A Comprehensive Collection of the Views of Thomas Jefferson*, (Funk and Wagnalls Company, 1900), 195.

103. James Madison, *The Federalist: A Commentary on the Constitution of the United States, Vol. 1, 51*, (New York: Dunne, 1901), 357.

104. John Stuart Mill, "Utilitarianism, Chapter 2: What Utilitarianism Is," *Utilitarianism.com*, http://www.utilitarianism.com/mill2.htm, (accessed on April 15, 2010).

105. Edward Gibbon, *The History of the Decline and Fall of the Roman Empire, Vol. 5, (*H. Frowde, Oxford University Press, 1907), 353.

NOTES

106. Carl Cavanagh Hodge and Cathal J. Nolan, *US Presidents and Foreign Policy,* (ABC-CLIO, 2007), 389.

107. Ibid.

108. John O'Sullivan, "Annexation", United States Magazine and Democratic Review 17, No.1 (1845): 5-10).

109. William E. Channing, *The Works of William E. Channing, D.D.*, (New York: American Unitarian Association, 1890), 760.

110. Sir Winston Churchill, *Never give in!:The Best of Winston Churchill's Speeches,* (Hyperion, 2003), 4.

111. James K. Polk, "Message on War with Mexico," *PBS*, May 11, 1846, http://www.pbs.org/weta/thewest/resources/archives/two/mexdec.htm.

112. Marion Mills Miller, *Great Debates in American History: Foreign Relations, Part 1*," (Current Literature Publication Co., 1913), 376.

113. Lynn Hudson Parson, *John Quincy Adams* (Lanham, Rowman & Littlefield Publishers, Inc., 2001), 265.

114. Ulysses S. Grant, *Personal Memoirs of Ulysses S. Grant* (New York, Cosimo, Inc., 2007) 16.

115. The American Presidency Project, "James K. Polk – Second Annual Message December 8, 1846," http://www.presidency.ucsb.edu/ws/index.php?pid=29487 (accessed on April 22, 2010).

116. John T. Woolley and Gerhard Peters, "James K. Polk – Second Annual Message December 8, 1846," *The American Presidency Online,* http://www.presidency.ucsb.edu/ws/index.php?pid=29487, (accessed on April 22, 2010).

117. "American President: Ulysses S. Grant, Domestic Affairs," *The Miller Center for Public Affairs*, http://millercenter.org/academic/americanpresident/grant/essays/biography/5 (accessed on April 22, 2010).

118. G W Townsend, *Memorial Life of William McKinley,* (READ Books, 2008), 157-158.

119. United States Department of State, *Papers Relating to the Foreign Relations of the United States,* (G.P.O., 1922), 755.

120. Richard F. Hamilton, *President McKinley, War and Empire: President McKinley and America's "New Empire,"* (Transaction Publishers, 2006), 80.

121. Wolfgang Kaleck, Center for Constitutional Rights, *International Prosecution of Human Rights Crimes,* (New York: Springer, 2007), 203-204.

122. Susan Brewer, *"Why America Fights: Patriotism and War Propaganda from the Philippines to Iraq,"* (Oxford University Press US, 2009), 26-27.

123. Ibid.

124. Ibid, (36).

125. Duke University, "South Atlantic Quarterly, Volume 20," (Duke University Press, 1921), 381.

126. *In* Holly Sklar, *Washington's War on Nicaragua,* (South End Press, 1988), 4.

127. "Dominican Republic, 1916-1924," *US State Department*, http://www.state.gov/r/pa/ho/time/wwi/108649.htm, (accessed on April 22, 2010).

128. Ibid.

129. Woodrow Wilson, "President Wilson's Great Speeches and Other History Making Documents," (Stanton and Van Vliet, 1917), 246-248.

130. Patrick O'Sullivan, *The Lusitania: Unraveling the Mysteries*, (Sheridan House, Inc., 2000), 130.

131. Ibid, (132-133)

132. "Kellogg-Briand Pact" *The Avalon Project*, Yale.edu, http://www.yale.edu/lawweb/avalon/imt/kbpact.htm (accessed April 15, 2010).

133. Donald E. Schmidt, *The Folly of War: American Foreign Policy 1828-2005*, (Algora Publishing, 2005), 173-174.

134. Ibid. (174)

135. John V. Denson, *Reassessing the Presidency: The Rise of the Executive State and the Decline of Freedom* (Ludwig von Mises Institute, 2001), 497.

136. Lester H. Brune, Richard Dean Burns, *Chronological History of U.S. Foreign Relations: 1932-1988*, (Routledge, 2003), 559.

137. Steven P. Meyer and Jeffrey Steinberg, "Henry Luce's Empire of Fascism", *EIR*, June 25 2004: http://www.larouchepub.com/other/2004/site_packages/3125ccf_luce.html (accessed April 19, 2010)

138. Henry Luce made the irrational nature of his desire to expand inarguable by writing: "It now becomes our time to be the powerhouse from which the ideals spread throughout the world and do their mysterious work of lifting the life of mankind from the level of the beasts to what the Psalmist called a little lower than the angels."(*In* Jonathan Yardley, "Jonathan Yardley reviews *The Publisher*, by Alan Brinkley", *Washington Post*, April 18 2010: http://www.washingtonpost.com/wp-dyn/content/article/2010/04/16/AR2010041602801.html)

CHAPTER 5

139. Sir Winston Churchill, *The End of the Beginning: War Speeches*, (Manchester: Ayer Co., 1977), 268.

140. George R. Goethals, *Encyclopedia of Leadership*, (Berkshire Publishing LLC, 2004), 1761.

141. Ibid.

142. Ibid.

143. Ibid.

144. Adam's speech lectured that while America was "the well-wisher to the freedom and independence of all," she would be "champion and vindicator only of her own" (John Quincy Adams,

"Speech to the U.S. House of Representatives on Foreign Policy (July 4, 1821)," *Mills Center of Public Affairs, UVA*, http://miller-center.org/scripps/archive/speeches/detail/3484, (accessed on April 15, 2010).

145. *In* Piers Brendon, *The Decline and Fall of the British Empire*, Random House, 2007, p. 113.

146. Philip P. Pan, "Georgia Set Off War, Probe Finds," October 1, 2009, http://www.washingtonpost.com/wp-dyn/content/article/2009/09/30/AR2009093004840.html, (accessed on April 21, 2010).

147. George Bush, "Bush: State of union is strong", *CNN.com* Jan. 23 2007, http://www.cnn.com/2007/POLITICS/01/23/sotu.bush.transcript/index.html, (accessed on April 15, 2010).

148. George Bush, "Transcript: President George Bush's Second Inaugural", *FoxNews.com*, Jan. 20, 2005, http://www.foxnews.com/politics/2009/01/17/transcript-president-george-w-bushs-second-inaugural/, (accessed on April 15, 2010).

149. Harry Truman, "President Harry S. Truman's Address Before A Joint Session of Congress, March 12th, 1947," The Avalon Project, *Law.Yale.edu*, http://avalon.law.yale.edu/20th_century/trudoc.asp (accessed on April 15, 2010).

150. George Washington expressly stated: "The great rule of conduct for us in regard to foreign nations is in extending our commercial relations, to have with them as little political connection as possible... Hence, therefore, it must be unwise in us to implicate ourselves by artificial ties in the ordinary vicissitudes of [the world's] politics, or the ordinary combinations and collisions of [international] friendships or enmities," (George Washington, "George Washington on Foreign Affairs *September 19, 1976," *Library of Virginia,* http://www.lva.virginia.gov/lib-edu/education/psd/nation/foreign.htm, (accessed on April 15, 2010).

151. According to the U.S. Department of Defense's statistics, between 33,000 and 37,000 lost their lives in the Korean War.

"U.S. Relations: The Korean War," *PBS*, October 19, 2006, http://www.pbs.org/newshour/indepth_coverage/asia/northkorea/relations.html (accessed on April 17, 2010).

152. President Eisenhower, "Address in New Orleans at the Ceremony Marking the 150th Anniversary of the Louisiana Purchase, October 7, 1953," http://www.eisenhowermemorial.org/speeches/19531007%20Address%20at%20150th%20Anniversary%20of%20the%20Louisiana%20Purchase.htm (accessed on April 15, 2010).

153. Michael T. Hayes, "The Republican Road Not Taken: The Foreign-Policy Vision of Robert A. Taft," *The Independent Review, Volume 8, Number 4, Spring 2004,* 518, http://www.independent.org/publications/tir/article.asp?a=37.

154. Jeffrey Miron, "Legalize Drugs to Stop Violence," *CNN*, March 24, 2009, http://www.cnn.com/2009/POLITICS/03/24/miron.legalization.drugs/index.html (accessed on April 21, 2010).

155. Jerry Taylor, "Time to Lay the 1973 Oil Embargo to Rest," *CATO Institute,* October 17, 2003, http://www.cato.org/pub_display.php?pub_id=3272 (accessed on April 22, 2010).

156. Ibid.

157. Ibid.

158. "Handshake with Obama Belies Chavez's Contempt for America," *Fox News*, April 20, 2009, http://www.foxnews.com/politics/first100days/2009/04/20/concerns-brewing-obamas-warm-embrace-chavez/ (accessed on December 17, 2009).

159. Council on Hemispheric Affairs, "The United States and Venezuela: More Than Just A Gun Show," August 12, 2008, available at: http://www.coha.org/2008/08/the-united-states-and-venezuela-the-gun-show/, (accessed on April 19, 2010).

160. Ibid.

161. Associated Press, "U.S.-Iran Trade Stronger Than Most Suspect," *Fox News*, July 8, 2009, http://www.foxnews.com/story/0,2933,378167,00.html.

162. Statistical Abstracts 1901-1950, *U.S. Census Bureau*, http://www.census.gov/prod/www/abs/statab1901-1950.htm, (accessed on April 19, 2010).

163. Ibid.

164. Exports are a crucial component when assessing GDP. When exports exceed imports, the GDP rises; when imports exceed exports, the GDP falls. While imports certainly provide a benefit to American consumers, they negatively affect United States prosperity, as measured by GDP; thus, an analysis of United States exports will suffice for this analysis. The insignificance of foreign direct investments into the United States also warrants its disregard. Further, the trend in exports is similar to imports. America's greatest sources of imports are #1 -China, #2 - Canada, #3 - Mexico, #4 - Japan, #5 - Germany, #6 - United Kingdom.

165. United States of America, "U.S. Export Fact Sheet," *U.S. Department of Commerce*, released February 11, 2009, available at: http://www.trade.gov/press/press_releases/2009/export-factsheet_021109.pdf; CIA Factbook, "United States," *CIA*, available at: https://www.cia.gov/library/publications/the-world-factbook/geos/us.html (accessed on April 22, 2010).

166. U.S. Census Bureau, Foreign Trade Statistics, http://www.census.gov/foreign-trade/statistics/highlights/top/top0812yr.html, (accessed on April 22, 2010).

167. Joseph Schumpeter, *Imperialism and Social Classes: Two Essays,* (Meridian Books, 1951), 51.

CHAPTER 6

168. Steven Casey, *Selling the Korean War*, (Oxford University Press, 2008), 28.

169. Franklin D. Mitchell, *Harry S. Truman and the news media*, (University of Missouri Press, 1998), 65.

NOTES

170. Ibid.

171. Paul M. Edwards, *The Korean War,* (Greenwood Press, 1988), 20-21.

172. John Dean, "Findlaw Forum: The President Needs Congressional Approval to Declare War on Iraq," *CNN*, August 30, 2002, http://archives.cnn.com/2002/LAW/08/columns/fl.dean.warpowers/ (Accessed on April 19, 2010).

173. Ibid.

174. *In* Arthur Meier Schesinger, *The Imperial Presidency*, (First Mariner Books, 2004), 133.

175. Ibid.

176. John Dean, "Findlaw Forum: The President Needs Congressional Approval to Declare War on Iraq," *CNN*, August 30, 2002, http://archives.cnn.com/2002/LAW/08/columns/fl.dean.warpowers/ (Accessed on April 19, 2010).

177. *In* Arthur V. Watkins, *The Western Political Quarterly*, Vol. 4, No. 4, December, 1951, 539-549.

178. UN Participation Act, December 20, 1945, The Avalon Project, Yale University, 2008, http://avalon.law.yale.edu/20th_century/decad031.asp, (accessed on April 19, 2010).

179. John Dean, "Findlaw Forum: The President Needs Congressional Approval to Declare War on Iraq," *CNN*, August 30, 2002, http://archives.cnn.com/2002/LAW/08/columns/fl.dean.warpowers/, (Accessed on April 19, 2010).

180. Ibid.

181. *In* Paul Krugman, "Games Nations Play," *New York Times*, 2003, http://www.nytimes.com/2003/01/03/opinion/games-nations-play.html?pagewanted=1, (accessed on April 19, 2010).

182. According to the U.S. Department of Defense's statistics, between 33,000 and 37,000 lost their lives in the Korean War. ("U.S. Relations: The Korean War," *PBS*, October 19, 2006, http://www.pbs.org/newshour/indepth_coverage/asia/northkorea/relations.html).

183. Lyndon Johnson, "Gulf of Tonkin Incident," August 4, 1964, http://usa.usembassy.de/etexts/speeches/rhetoric/lbjgulf. htm, (accessed on April 19, 2010).

184. Microsoft Encarta, "Johnson's Gulf of Tonkin Message," http://encarta.msn.com/sidebar_761594754/Johnson's_Gulf_of_Tonkin_Message.html, (accessed on April 22, 2010).

185. Marvin E. Gettleman, *Vietnam and America: A Documented History*, (Grove Press, 1995), 247.

186. "Gulf of Tonkin, 1964: Perspectives From Lyndon Johnson and Military Command Center Tapes," *Miller Center of Public Affairs, UVA*, http://www.whitehousetapes.net/exhibit/gulf-tonkin-1964-perspectives-lyndon-johnson-and-national-military-command-center-tapes, (accessed on April 19, 2010).

187. Ibid.

188. Eric Alterman, *When President Lie*, (Penguin Books, 2004), 188.

189. Tom Wells, *The War Within: America's battle for Vietnam*, (iUniverse, 2001), 11.

190. James Irdell, "Proceedings and Debates of the Convention of North-Carolina," *UNC-Chapel Hill*, 1788, http://millercenter.org/scripps/archive/speeches/detail/4032, (accessed April 19, 2010).

191. Lyndon Baines Johnson, "Statement on Sending Troops to the Dominican Republic," *Mills Center for Public Affairs, UVA*, 1965, http://millercenter.org/scripps/archive/speeches/detail/4032, (accessed April 19, 2010).

192. Randall Bennett Woods, *J. William Fulbright, Vietnam, and the search for a cold war foreign policy*, (Cambridge University press, 1998), 98-99.

193. Ibid.

194. John Dumbrell, *President Lyndon Johnson and Soviet communism*, (Manchester University Press, 2004), p.146

195. Russell Crandall, *Gunboat Democracy*, (Rowan and Littlefield, 2006), 71.

196. Lyndon Johnson, "Radio and Television Report to the American People on the Situation in the Dominican Republic," *UCSB: The American Presidency Project,* May 2nd, 1965, http://www.presidency.ucsb.edu/mediaplay.php?id=26932&admin=36 (accessed on April 21, 2010).

197. John Dumbrell, *President Lyndon Johnson and Soviet Communism*, Manchester University Press, 2004, p.147

198. William Blum, *Killing Hope*, (Zed Books, 2003), 183.

199. Ibid. (182)

200. Leon Friedman, "Watergate and afterward," (Hofstra University, 1992), 222.

201. Ibid.

202. James P. Pfiffner, *The Character Factor*, (Texas A&M University Press, 2004), 55.

203. Arthur Meier Schlesinger, *The Imperial Presidency*, (First Mariner Books, 2004), 357.

204. Ibid.

205. Rick Perlstein, *Nixonland*, (Scribner, 2008), 362.

206. Bill Clinton, "Transcript of the President's Speech on Bosnia", *CNN*, 1955, http://www.cnn.com/US/9511/bosnia_speech/speech.html, (accessed on April 22, 2010).

207. James P. Pfiffner, "Did President Bush Mislead the Country in his Arguments for War with Iraq?" *George Mason University*, http://gunston.gmu.edu/pfiffner/index_files/Page2451.htm, (accessed on April 22, 2010).

208. Sue Chan, "Bush Administration Links Iraq, Al Qaeda," *CBS*, http://www.cbsnews.com/stories/2002/09/26/national/main523326.shtml, (accessed on April 24, 2010).

209. Jamie McIntyre, "Rumsfeld: Al Qaeda comments 'misunderstood'", CNN, http://edition.cnn.com/2004/WORLD/meast/10/04/rumsfeld.iraq/ (accessed on April 24, 2010).

210. James P. Pfiffner, "Did President Bush Mislead the Country in his Arguments for War with Iraq?" *George Mason University*,

http://gunston.gmu.edu/pfiffner/index_files/Page2451. htm, (accessed on April 24, 2010).

211. Ibid.

212. BBC, "White House 'warned over Iraq claim'", *BBC*, July 9, 2003, http://news.bbc.co.uk/2/hi/americas/3056626.stm, (accessed April 21, 2010).

213. James P. Pfiffner, "Did President Bush Mislead the Country in his Arguments for War with Iraq?" *George Mason University*, http://gunston.gmu.edu/pfiffner/index_files/Page2451. htm, (accessed on April 24, 2010).

214. Speech at the University of Cambridge, England, May 26, 1910 *in* Candice Millard, *The River of Doubt: Theodore Roosevelt's Darkest Journey*, (Broadway Books, 2005), 18.

215. James Madison, "Political Observations," April 20, 1795 in *Letters and Other Writings of James Madison, Volume IV*, 491.

216. Letter from Thomas Jefferson to James Madison (Sept. 6, 1789) *in* Thomas Jefferson, *The Papers of Thomas Jefferson*, (Julian P. Boyd ed., 1958), 392, 397.

217. Dana Priest, "U.S. military teams, intelligence deeply involved in aiding Yemen on strikes," *Washington Post*, Jan. 17, 2010, http://www.washingtonpost.com/wp-dyn/content/article/2010/01/26/AR2010012604239. html?hpid=topnews, (accessed on April 15, 2010).

CHAPTER 7

218. John Yoo, "Memorandum for William J. Haynes II, General Counsel of the Department of Defense," 14 March 2003, http://www.aclu.org/files/pdfs/safefree/yoo_army_torture_memo.pdf, (accessed on April 21, 2010).

219. "Executive Order—Ensuring Lawful interrogations," The White House, 22 January 2009, http://www.whitehouse.

gov/the_press_office/EnsuringLawfulInterrogations/, (accessed 5 March 2010).

220. James Madison, "Political Observation," in *Letters and Other Writings of James Madison, vol.2* (Philadelphia: J.B. Lippincott & co., 1865), Vol. IV, 491.

221. Alexander Hamilton, John Jay, and James Madison, *The Federalist Papers* (University of Virginia, 1788), Section 8, Electronic Text Center, http://etext.lib.virginia.edu/toc/modeng/public/HMJFedr.html, (accessed 29 January 2010).

222. "Military Commissions Act of 2006," *United States Department of Defense*, 17 October 2006, http://frwebgate.access.gpo.gov/cgi-bin/getdoc.cgi?dbname=109_cong_public_laws&docid=f:publ366.109.pdf (accessed 17 February 2010).

223. David Keene, "Enemy Combatants—Maybe," *The Hill*, 5 October 2009, http://thehill.com/opinion/columnists/david-keene/61689-enemy-combatants-maybe (accessed 5 March 2010).

224. Christopher Drew, "Drones Are Weapons of Choices in Fighting Qaeda," *New York Times*, 16 March 2009, http://www.nytimes.com/2009/03/17/business/17uav.html (accessed 17 February 2010).

225. David Kilcullen & Andrew McDonald Exum, "Death from Above, Outrage Down Below," *New York Times*, 16 May 2009, http://www.nytimes.com/2009/05/17/opinion/17exum.html (accessed 17 February 2010).

226. Philip B. Kurland and Ralph Lerner, eds., "James Madison to W.T. Barry, 4 August 1822," *The Founder's Constitution,* (Chicago: University of Chicago Press, 1987), http://press pubs.uchicago.edu/founders/documents/v1ch18s35.html, (accessed 5 March 2010).

227. "Daily Compilation of Presidential Documents, 2009 DCPD No. 200900359", *United States Office of the Federal Register*, http://www.gpoaccess.gov/presdocs/2009/DCPD-200900359.htm, (accessed 17 February 2010).

228. David Morgan, "Clinton Says U.S. Could "Totally Obliterate" Iran," *Reuters*, 22 April 2008, http://www.reuters.com/article/idUSN2224332720080422 (accessed 5 March 2010).

229. "Full Text of Obama's Nobel Peace Prize Speech," *MSNBC*, 10 December 2009, http://www.msnbc.msn.com/id/34360743/ (accessed 5 March 2010).

230. Alexander Hamilton, *The Federalist No. 69:The Real Character of the Executive*, *Constitution.org*, March 14, 1788, http://www.constitution.org/fed/federa69.htm (accessed on April 18, 2010).

231. Barak Obama, "Remarks by the President in Address to the Nation on the Way Forward in Afghanistan and Pakistan," The White House, Office of the Press Secretary, 1 December 2009, http://www.whitehouse.gov/the-press-office/remarks-president-address-nation-way-forward-afghanistan-and-pakistan, (accessed 17 February 2010).

232. John G. Nicolay & John Hay eds, "Letter to William H. Herndon, 15 February 1848," in *The Complete Works of Abraham Lincoln*, *vol. 2* (New York: Francis D. Tandy Company, 1894).

233. Barack Obama, "Address to the Nation on the Way Forward in Afghanistan and Pakistan." Remarks, Eisenhower Hall Theatre, United States Military Academy at West Point, West Point, New York, 1 December 2009, http://www.whitehouse.gov/the-press-office/remarks-president-address-nation-way-forward-afghanistan-and-pakistan (accessed 5 March 2010).

234. "Full Text of Obama's Nobel Peace Prize Speech," *MSNBC*, 10 December 2009, http://www.msnbc.msn.com/id/34360743/ (accessed 5 March 2010).

235. *In* David Cho, "A Skeptical Outsider Becomes Bush's 'Wartime General'," *Washington Post*, 19 November 2008. http://www.washingtonpost.com/wp-dyn/content/article/2008/11/18/AR2008111803938.html (accessed 19 February 2010).

236. Ibid.

NOTES

237. The Constitution of Japan, Chapter 2, Article 2, "The Renunciation of War", *The Solon Law Archive*, http://www.so-lon.org/Constitutions/Japan/English/english-Constitution.html (accessed April 18, 2010).

CHAPTER 8

238. *In* Aaron Klein, *Striking Back: The 1972 Munich Massacre and Israel's Deadly Response*, (Random House, 2007), 141.
239. William Shakespeare, *The Complete Works of William Shakespeare: King Henry IV, Part I,* (Boston: Gin, Heath & Co., 1881), 73.
240. The Pentagon Papers, Volume 2, Chapter 2, "The Strategic Hamlet Program", (Boston: Beacon Press, 1971).

CHAPTER 9

241. William Shakespeare, *The Complete Works of William Shakespeare: Julius Caesar*, (Boston: Gin Heath & Co., 1881), Act I, Scene ii, ln. 141-147.
242. Edward R. Murrow, "A Report on Senator Joseph R. McCarthy," See it Now, *CBS-TV*, March 9th, 1954, http://www.lib.berke-ley.edu/MRC/murrowmccarthy.html (accessed on April 22, 2010).
243. Ralph Waldo Emerson, "Essays: First Series, 1841," *UVA Library*, http://etext.virginia.edu/etcbin/toccer-new2?id=EmeEssF.sgm&images=images/modeng&data=/texts/english/mod-eng/parsed&tag=public&part=1&division=div1 (accessed on April 22, 2010).

Author Biography

Bruce Fein is a nationally and internationally renowned constitutional lawyer, scholar and writer. After graduating from the Harvard Law School with honors in 1972, Mr. Fein served as special assistant to the Assistant Attorney General for the Office of Legal Counsel at the U.S. Department of Justice from 1973-1975. The lion's share of his work consisted of providing constitutional advice to the White House and executive branch agencies and drafting congressional testimony. He also authored a monograph on the definition of an impeachable offense as envisioned by the Constitution's makers in conjunction with the House Judiciary Committee's impeachment hearings against President Richard M. Nixon.

From 1975-1976, Mr. Fein served as Assistant Director in the Office of Legal Policy at the U.S. Department of Justice where his primary duties concerned legislative initiatives aimed at upgrading the administration of federal justice. From 1981-1982, he served as Associate Deputy Attorney General in the U.S. Department of Justice and supervised the Department's litigation and vetting of candidates for the federal judiciary. He then became General Counsel of the Federal Communications Commission from 1983-1984, spearheading the repeal of the Fairness Doctrine as violating the free speech rights of broadcasters and re-architecting the telecommunications landscape after Judge Greene's Modified Final Judgment vivisecting AT&T. Mr. Fein was also appointed as Research Director for the House Republicans on the Joint Congressional Committee on Covert Arms Sales to Iran from 1986-1987.

Mr. Fein served as a Visitor Scholar for Constitutional Studies at the Heritage Foundation, an adjunct scholar at the American Enterprise Institute, and taught as an adjunct professor at George Washington University in Washington, D.C. Between 1985 and 2009, Mr. Fein wrote weekly Commentary Columns for *The Washington Times* on legal and international issues. Additionally, he wrote occasional guest articles for *The New York Times, Washington Post, Financial Times, USA Today, the American Bar Association Journal, Harvard Law Review*, and *Boston Globe* publications. He regularly appears on national television and radio, including MSNBC, FOX News, C-SPAN, BBC, Reuters, and NPR.

44438822R00143